Magdalene
Odundo

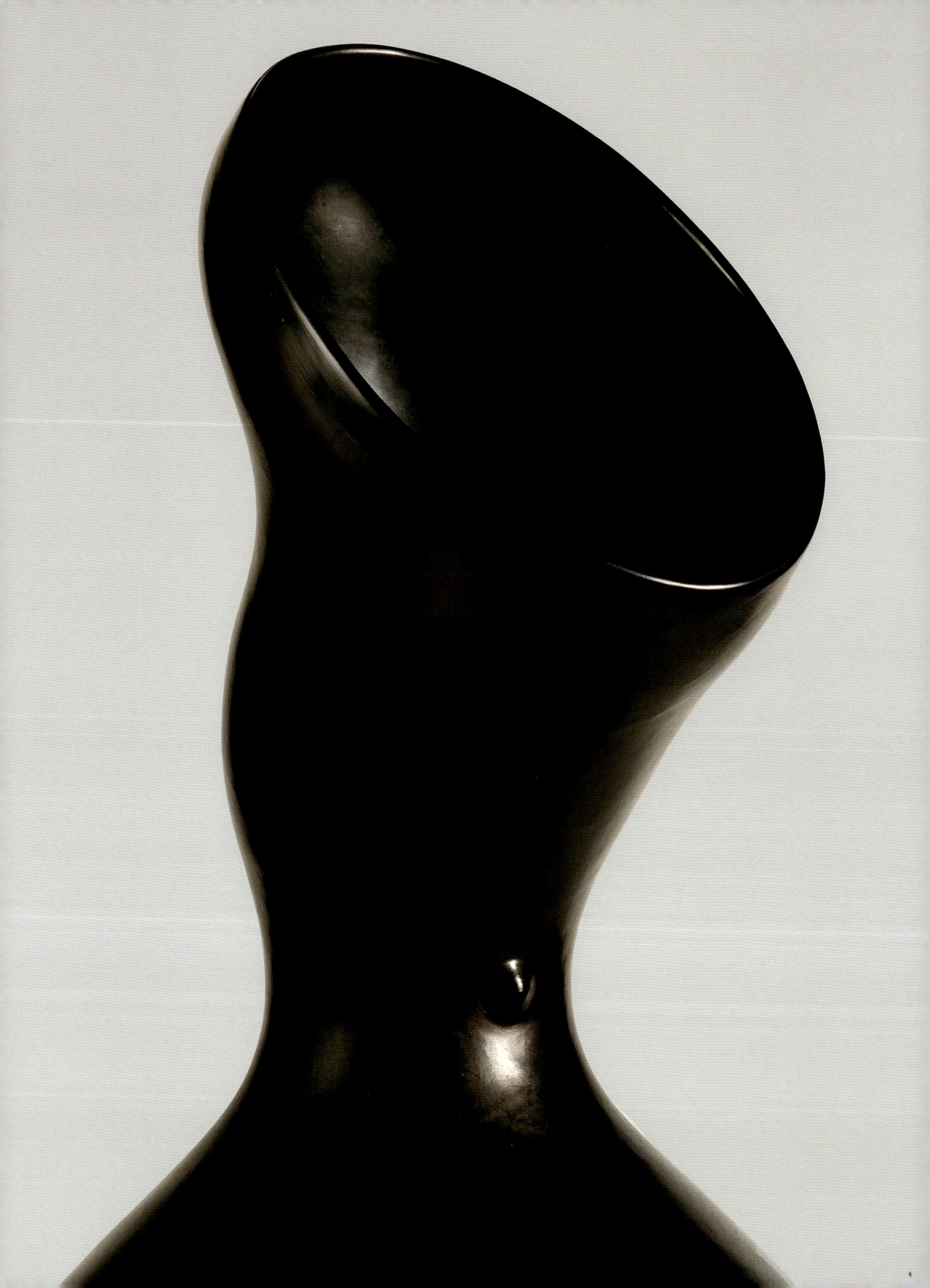

Magdalene Odundo

A Dialogue with Objects

Edited by Sequoia Miller

Gardiner Museum, Toronto

in association with
Princeton University Press,
Princeton and Oxford

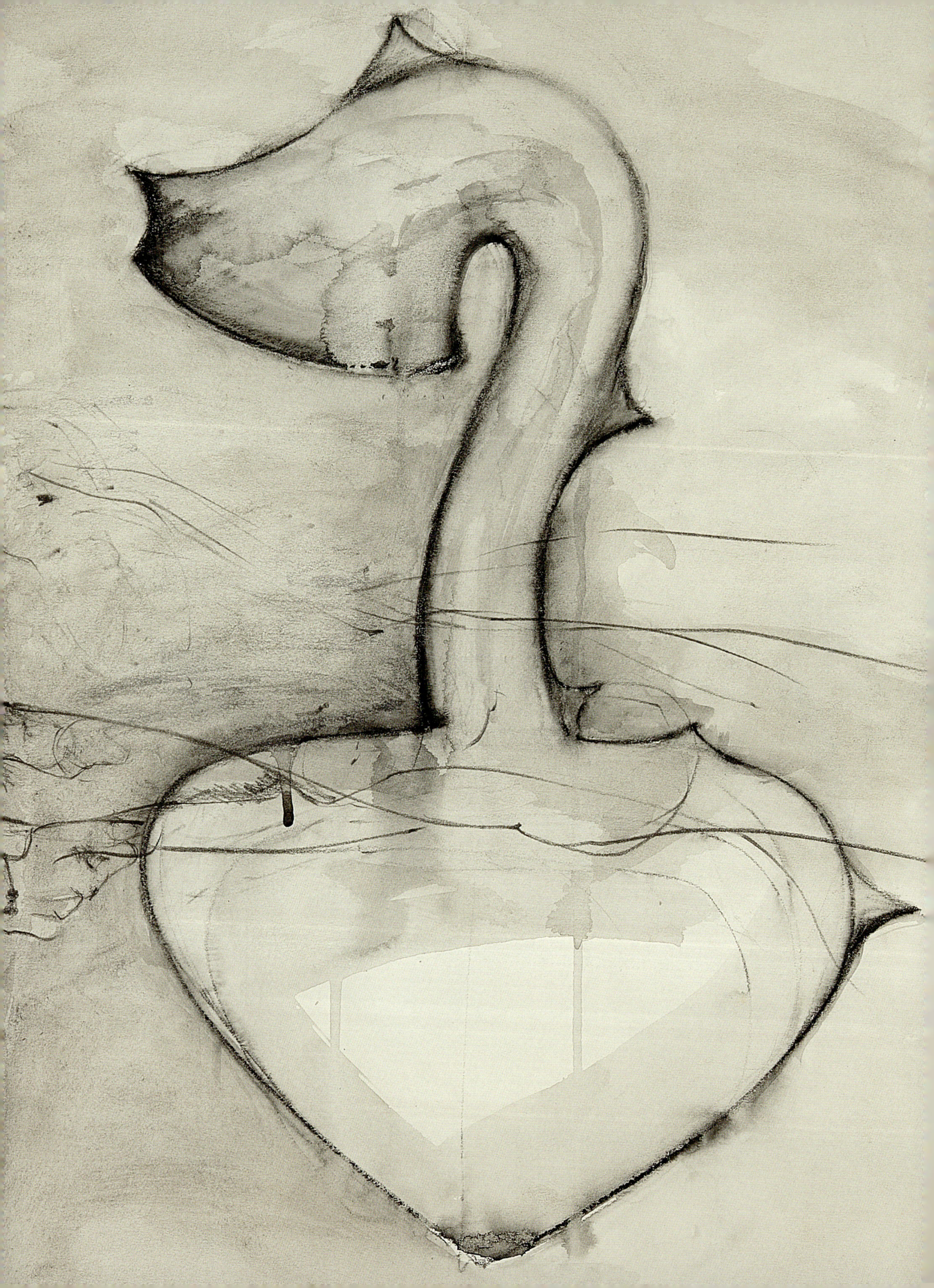

Contents

Susan Jefferies

Foreword

I first met Magdalene Odundo more than forty years ago while I was
on sabbatical in the UK. I noticed a small image of one of her pots in
a glossy magazine, and my husband, Bob, and I tracked her down
in Ripley, a village in Surrey, where she was living. From that first
encounter, my admiration for her artwork has grown and deepened,
as has our friendship. Over the years we have spent many memora-
ble times together, both personal and professional: laughing over
our children's antics, going to exhibitions, and visiting with ceramic
artists in North America and the UK, including Roseline Delisle,
Ruth Duckworth, Liz Fritsch, Jennifer Lee, and John Mason. The
array of experiences we have shared has enriched my thinking
about art and life. I know that Magdalene, not only as an artist but
also as an outstanding educator and mentor, has influenced
countless others as well.

The Gardiner Museum first brought Magdalene to Toronto in
1994, in collaboration with the Royal Ontario Museum, to speak at
the annual Decorative Arts Symposium and workshops, where she
gave a wise and warm presentation about growing up in Africa. In
2003, thanks to the generosity of Neal Roberts, the Museum was
able to purchase a very important and beautiful piece of her work,
a first for the Gardiner and for Canada. It was given in memory of
Susanne Roberts, an accomplished production potter who worked
in Britain, the United States, and Toronto. During my tenure as
curator, I was excited to bring Magdalene to the Gardiner again
for a workshop in 2006. Those who attended will never forget her

technique, working large, luscious coils of clay to form a pot in the style of the legendary Nigerian potter Ladi Kwali.

I am full of admiration for the way Magdalene engages in a relentless search for the essence of things, whether of ideas or objects. She does this by continually exploring and varying her forms. It is the nuance and the hints of other things, historical and cultural, that enhance the beauty and richness of her work. I love the art part, the nitty-gritty in her forms: the scale, the heartfelt line, the swelling volume, and the blooming surface. I've spent decades contemplating her work, and yet mysterious and unknowable aspects remain.

Always, there was the dream of a Magdalene Odundo exhibition at the Gardiner Museum, and now it has happened thanks to Sequoia Miller and his team. It brings me great pleasure to see the long association between the artist and the Gardiner continue with the presentation of this exhibition and book.

In this publication we are fortunate to have exciting and well-considered essays about Magdalene Odundo's art and her craft. Along with the many ideas proposed by these contributors, I would urge you to consider your own findings. As with any legitimate work of art, there is always more.

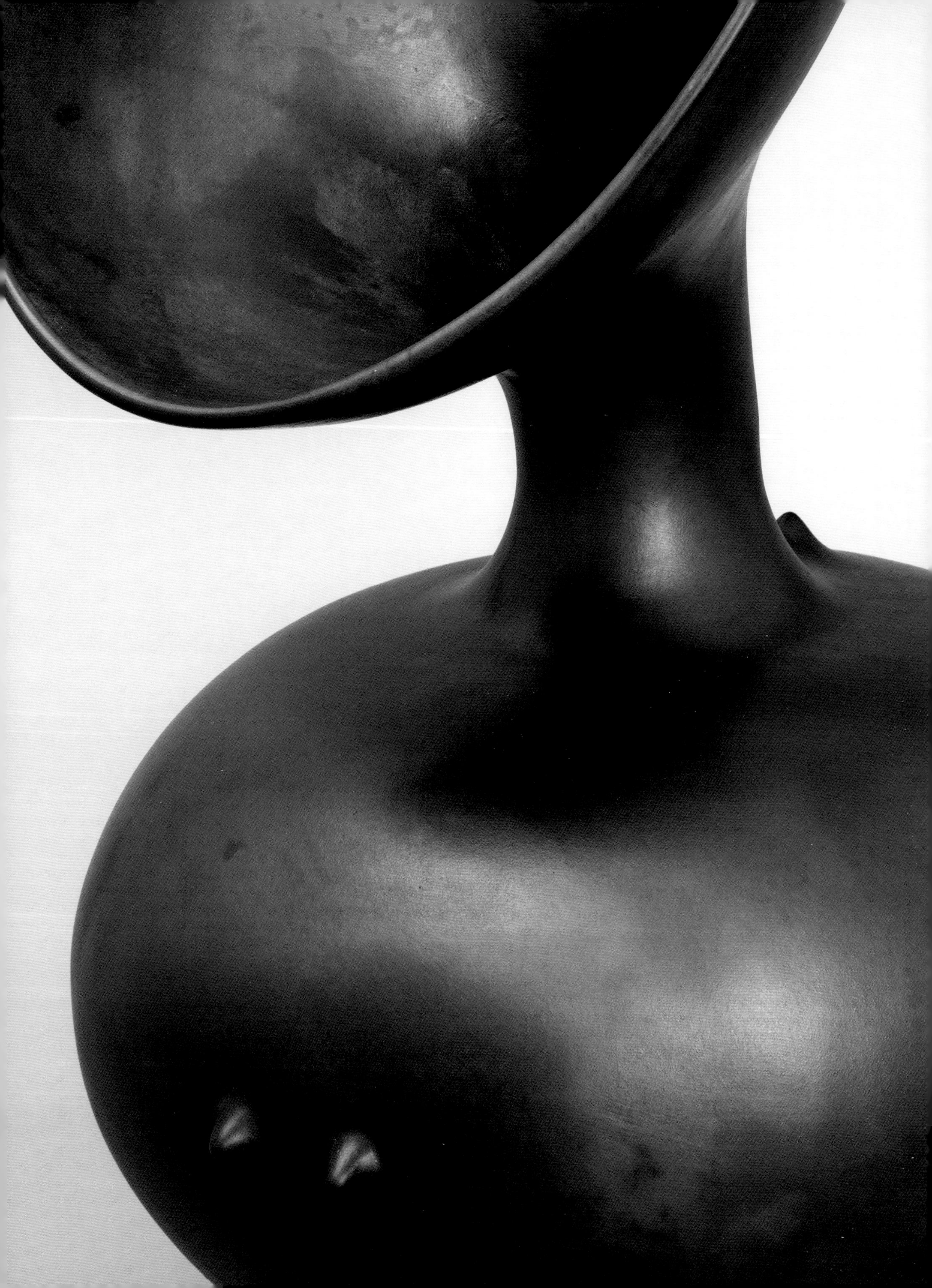

Sequoia Miller

Synthesis and Silence
Magdalene Odundo's Postcoloniality

Over the last forty years, Magdalene Odundo has rigorously pursued the affective power of the pared-down, refined ceramic vessel, at once intimate, evocative, and opaque (fig. 5). Often appreciated for their aesthetic sophistication and synthesis of world traditions, her sculpture and curatorial interventions also demonstrate a way of working transculturally that resists hierarchies of value and colonial imperatives. She began formulating this method of working across cultures early in her career through exposure to global museum collections, research, and travel. These cross-cultural connections have become more explicit through a series of exhibitions featuring her sculpture alongside art and artefacts from the recent and distant past that have inspired her.[1] Seen together, these projects help reveal the ways in which Odundo's work honours diverse knowledge systems and emphasizes our shared humanity, while rejecting structures of domination. Without explicitly thematizing political content in her work, Odundo shows a new model for working through colonial structures to achieve anti-colonial ends. With developments in postcolonial and Black feminist discourses in recent years, the political aspects of her methodology are only now coming into greater focus. Odundo and her work embody a path forward by actively modelling a more equitable system of cultural relation, one from which we can all learn.

Odundo's complex relationship with museum collections began in earnest when she left her native Kenya in 1971 to study in the

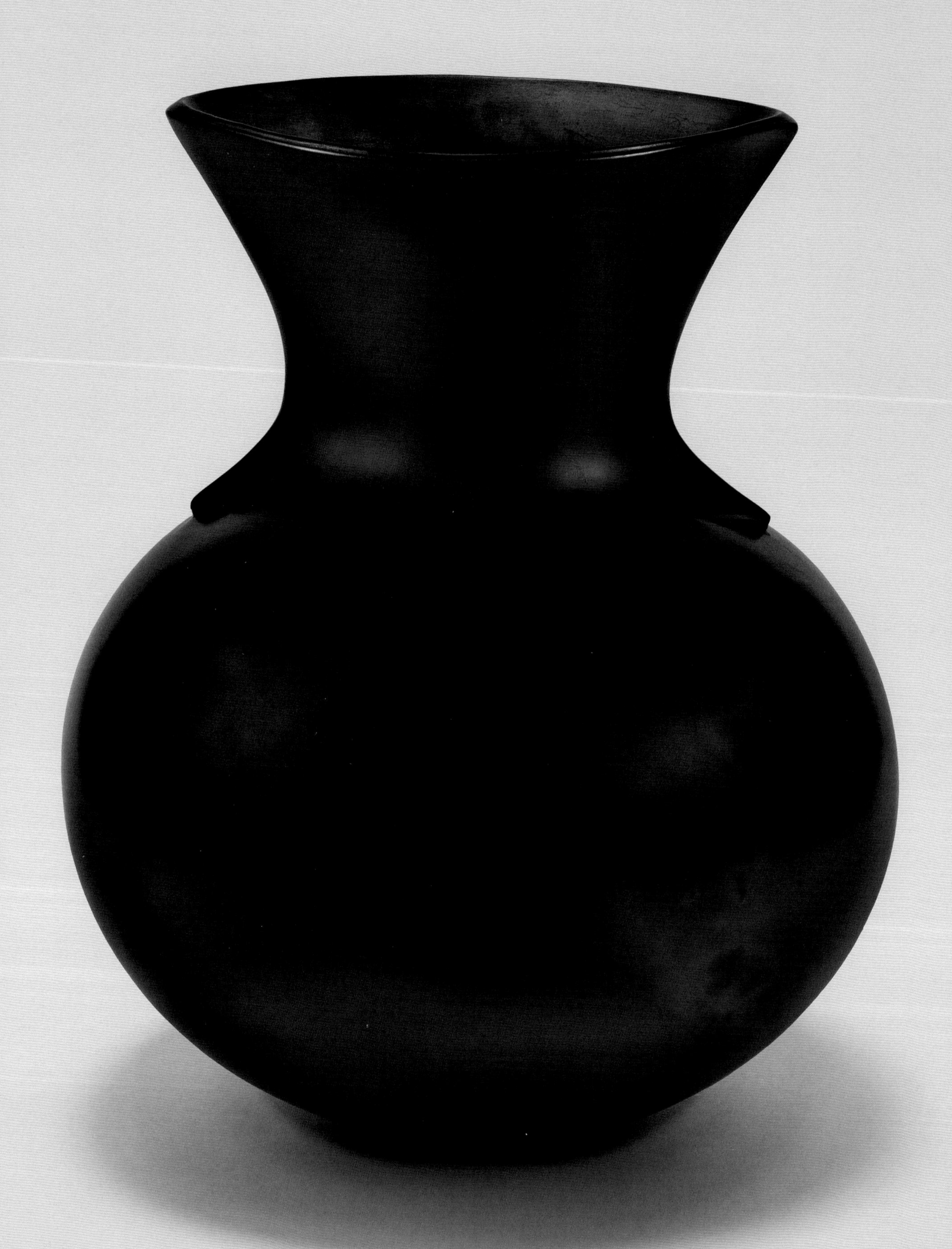

United Kingdom.[2] She had attended the Nairobi Polytechnic Institute and worked in graphic and signage design, yet sought further education. She enrolled in the Cambridge College of Art, where she focused on commercial art but was soon drawn towards ceramics, printmaking, and other fine art disciplines.[3] At Cambridge, Odundo began visiting museums regularly as sources of inspiration and information, including the Museum of Archaeology and Anthropology, the Fitzwilliam Museum, and Kettle's Yard. At the Museum of Archaeology and Anthropology, she encountered works from many global cultures, particularly those of Oceania and pre-Hispanic Americas. The Fitzwilliam introduced her to European fine and decorative art, including classical Greek vases and later European painting, as well as Islamic art and the highly refined Kerma ware of ancient Nubia. Kettle's Yard, a museum of modern and contemporary art, included continental modernists like Constantin Brancusi and Joan Miró alongside British artists such as Barbara Hepworth and Henry Moore.[4] Odundo was particularly taken with the work of Henri Gaudier-Brzeska, whose sculpture *Bird Swallowing a Fish* (1914) she initially mistook for being African rather than European.[5]

Seeing a wider range of African art and learning of its importance to early twentieth-century European artists, Odundo reconsidered her understanding of African cultural production: "I was taught that African art was primitive, and it was only when I later moved to the UK that I realized that this wasn't the case, and that the rest of the world was fascinated by the art of the African continent."[6] These early museum experiences were critical for Odundo in building her sense of self as an artist, as well as her understanding of the connections between cultures, both non-Western and Western. While the colonial origin of many of these collections was known, it was Odundo's position as an African woman and postcolonial subject that facilitated her ability to see cultures in relation to each other rather than within a hierarchy of value.

Odundo was born in Nairobi, the English-speaking capital of colonial Kenya, and raised in Mombasa, on the Kenyan coast, while attending Catholic schools. On holidays and summer vacations, she would return to her ancestral "reserve" in western Kenya, where she would carry out more traditional practices and speak in the local language, Lunyala.[7] As she describes, "Going between the colonial city and life on the reserve felt like living in two different worlds and having one foot in each."[8] Her evocation of two identities calls to mind W. E. B. Du Bois's notion of double consciousness, and the gap between the inner life of a Black person and awareness of how they are perceived externally in a racialized society.[9] Franz Fanon, in *Black Skin, White Masks*, similarly theorized the tensions within the colonized subject, navigating between their (often dissociated) native culture and that of the colonizer.[10] For Odundo, the phenomenon of living in two worlds became amplified when she moved to England, a relocation that began as temporary but became permanent. This life between cultures would become

Fig. 1 Magdalene Odundo, *Untitled*, 1984. Ceramic, 29 × 23 × 23 cm. Maxine and Stuart Frankel Foundation for Art

central to her art, allowing her to see cultural expression as relative while giving her the distance from her ancestral culture to approach it flexibly. Odundo's visionary leap was to see herself in each of these modes of expression and to synthesize them.

Odundo was also connecting with a wider Black and expatriate African community in Cambridge. A focal point for the Black community there was the Centre of African Studies, founded in 1965 as a gathering place for students at the university working in various departments on African material, as well as for visiting students and scholars.[11] The Centre created a sense of community for Odundo and deepened her exposure to the emerging field of postcolonial thought and the Black power movement in the United States. Writers such as James Baldwin, Angela Davis, Fanon, and Léopold Sédar Senghor helped expand Odundo's thinking about politics, colonialism, and Black diasporic identity. These ideas would come to inform how she looked at objects of both African and other origin as sources of inspiration, as well as the way she navigated her own position in British culture.[12]

Having transferred to the West Surrey College of Art and Design (now the University for the Creative Arts) in 1973, where she would eventually return as a longtime faculty member, Odundo traveled with her fellow students to visit eminent potters Bernard Leach (1887–1979) in Cornwall and Michael Cardew (1901–1983) in Devon.[13] Leach was highly influential as a founder of the studio pottery movement in England, known as much for his writings as for his ceramics.[14] He advocated for a return to handcraft, venerating East Asian ceramic traditions as a new standard for Western potters and presenting himself as a cultural bridge between East and West.[15] While Odundo admired Leach's cross-cultural approach, Cardew would prove to have the larger impact. Educated in classics at Cambridge, Cardew had been Leach's first apprentice and lived in Africa for fifteen years, where he ran colonial pottery enterprises in Ghana and Nigeria. He established the Abuja Pottery Training Centre in Abuja (now Suleja) in 1950 as a development enterprise, combining local skills with Western material technology to produce handmade ceramics for regional consumption and export.[16] The leading figure at the Training Centre was Ladi Kwali (c. 1925–1984), a gifted Gbagyi potter who had arrived in 1954 as a skilled artisan and went on to make sculpture combining local and Western idioms (fig. 2).

Odundo spent a transformative summer learning from Kwali and others at the Training Centre in 1974.[17] At Abuja, she adopted the traditional Gwari forming technique of opening a solid mound of clay with one's hands and building up the walls as one walks backwards around the stationary work. This method, connected to a matrilineal history of vessel making, was adaptable to different circumstances and personalities. Kwali represented a way of working that was grounded in a particular history yet also com-pletely contemporary. Another significant aspect of Odundo's experience there was her introduction to an apprenticeship model of learning. At West Surrey College, she was embedded in the

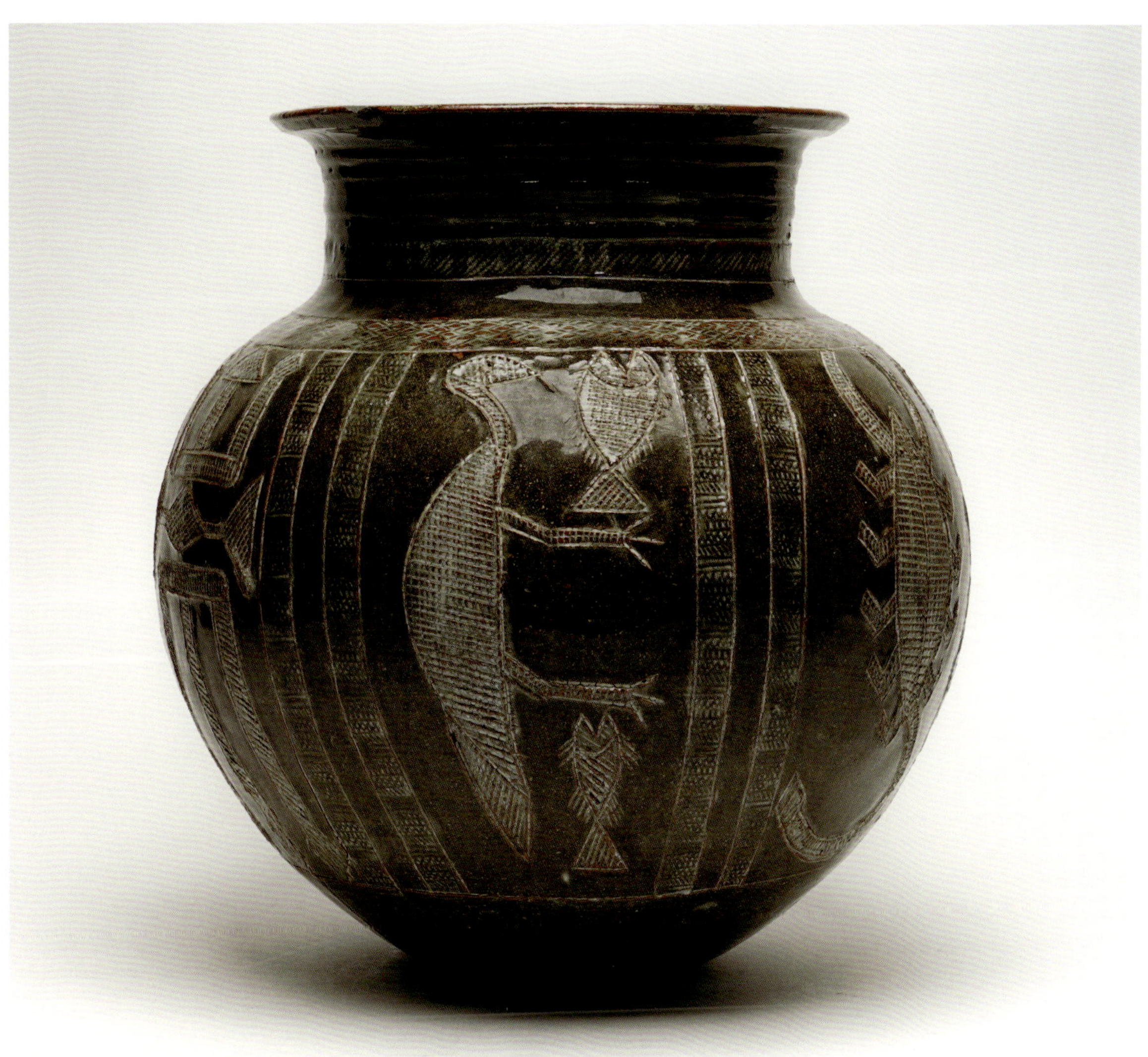

Fig. 2 Ladi Kwali, Jar, 1963. Stoneware, glaze, 36 × 35.5 × 35.5 cm. Gardiner Museum

academic arts curriculum as it had developed during the post–World War II decades with foundation courses, art history requirements, and critiques.[18] At Abuja, the emphasis was on close observation of makers and replication of techniques, requiring an acute sensitivity on the part of the student.[19] This approach honed Odundo's skill at close looking, which she would extend into other contexts, including both her later university-based teaching and how she works with museum objects, seeking connections across cultures and temporalities.

Odundo returned to Kenya in 1975 to research her own ancestral traditions. Her thesis for West Surrey focused on ritual ceramics in ethnic Abanyala communities, for which Odundo interviewed and observed women potters, studying how they made vessels for ceremonial occasions such as births, marriages, and funerals. Titled *Rites of Passage*, this work centered on objects that were already deeply imprinted in Odundo's mind, yet she brought to them newly acquired academic and analytic tools. The project deepened her appreciation for the symbolic function of ceramic vessels as containers for spiritual intention and aspiration, and as markers in the life cycle. Building on her experiences in museums and art schools in the UK, as well as at Abuja, this time in Kenya highlighted for Odundo the human need to invest meaning in ceramic objects and clay's capacity to sustain such content.

As a final ingredient, art history courses at West Surrey supplemented Odundo's travel and studio experiences. While some course readings upheld the framework of "primitivism" that held African art within a conventionally racist Western context, others advanced postcolonial scholarship, building upon earlier readings and discussions at the Centre of African Studies that called into question the centrality and dominance of Western culture.[20] Taken together, the deep intermixture of cultural forms and traditions evident in Odundo's mature studio practice emerged from her deliberate synthesis of Western and non-Western museum collections, academic and apprenticeship studio learning, direct ethnographic research, and postcolonial theory. A visit in 1976 to the United States, where she met Indigenous San Ildefonso Pueblo potter Maria Martinez (1887–1980), would expand her exposure to include direct experience with Native American traditions, yet her core structure of working transculturally was intact by the mid-1970s.

Odundo's deep understanding of how symbolic meanings are embedded in objects—be they art or artefact, ritual or quotidian, contemporary or ancient—equips her to distil a vast range of source material while retaining the integrity of the original objects and their cultures of production. Her complex synthesis of diverse influences into a singular artistic expression can be seen in a vessel from 2003 (fig. 5). The form consists of two volumes: a swelling, near-spherical shape on the bottom and an expansive, extravagantly flaring conical form above. The piece is relaxed yet poised, with elegant curves evocative of natural objects such as gourds,

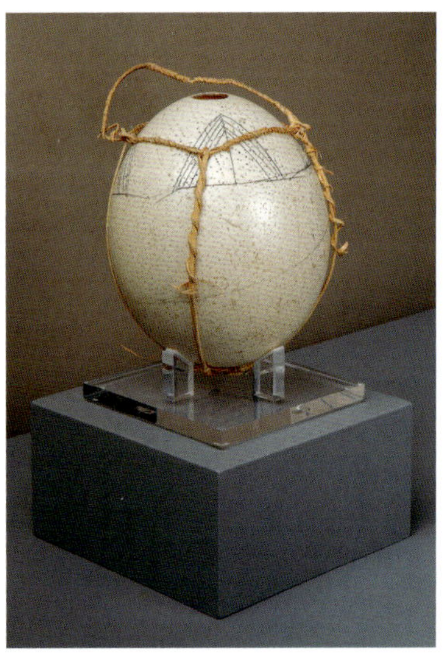

Fig. 3 Unidentified San artist, Decorated Egg, Ghanzi, Botswana, mid-20th century. Ostrich eggshell, fibre, grass, 16 × 12.5 cm. Royal Ontario Museum

Fig. 4 Unknown Artist, Pot, Kenya, 1960s. Unglazed ceramic, 23 × 34 × 34 cm. Gardiner Museum

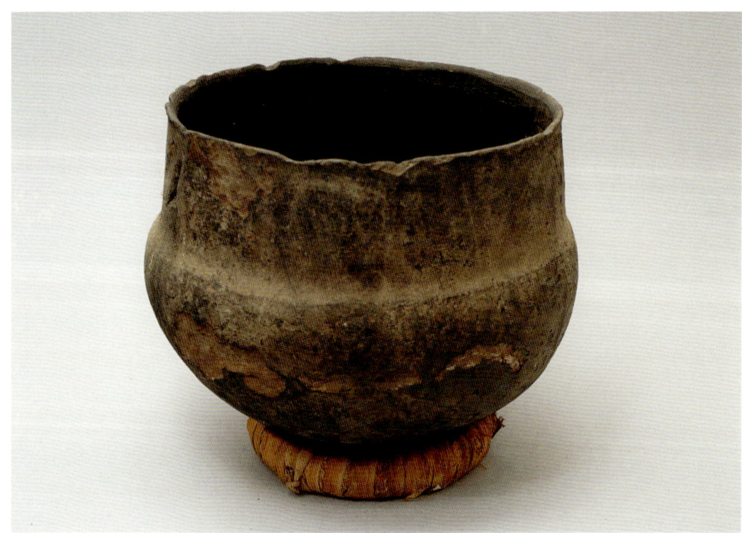

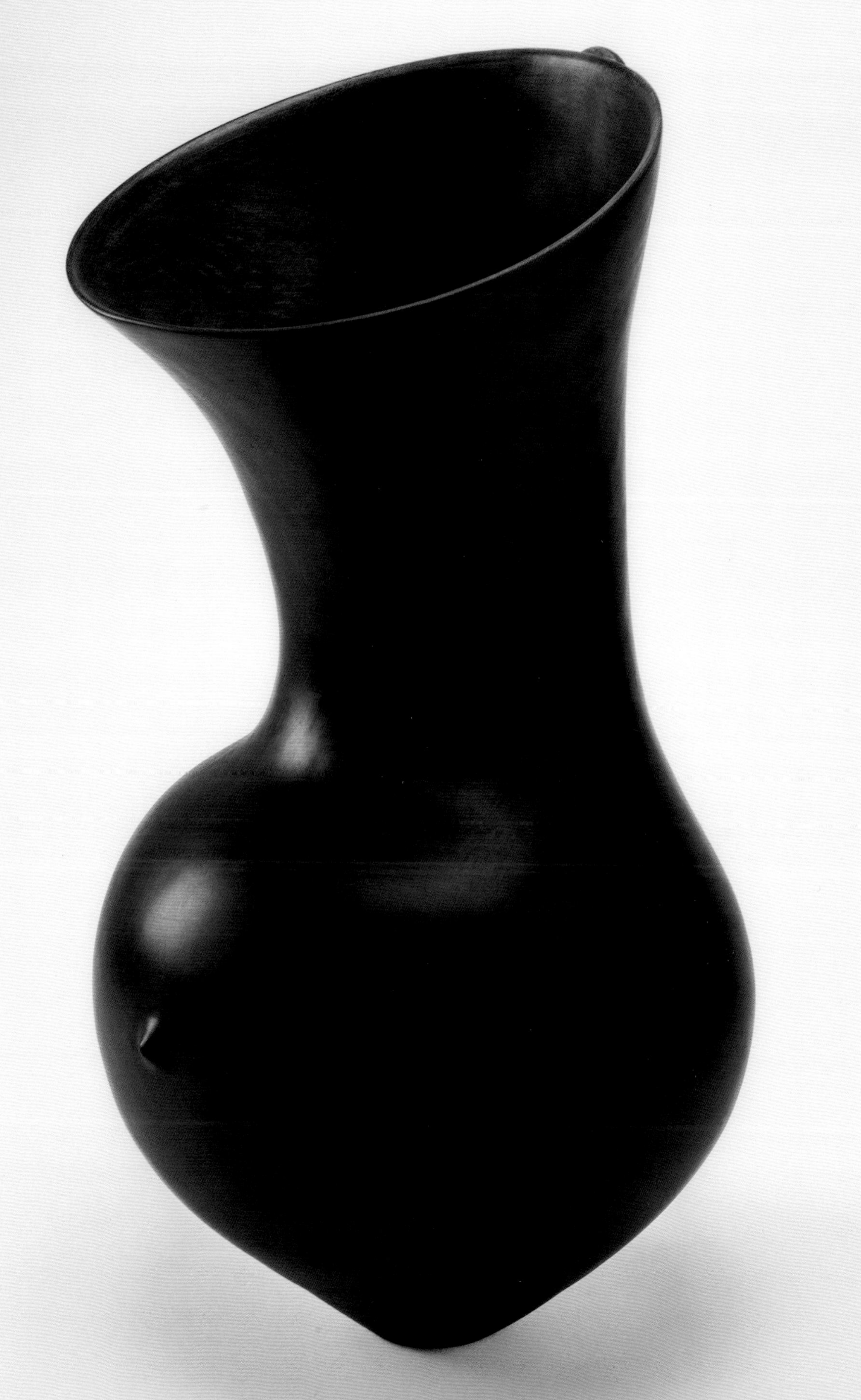

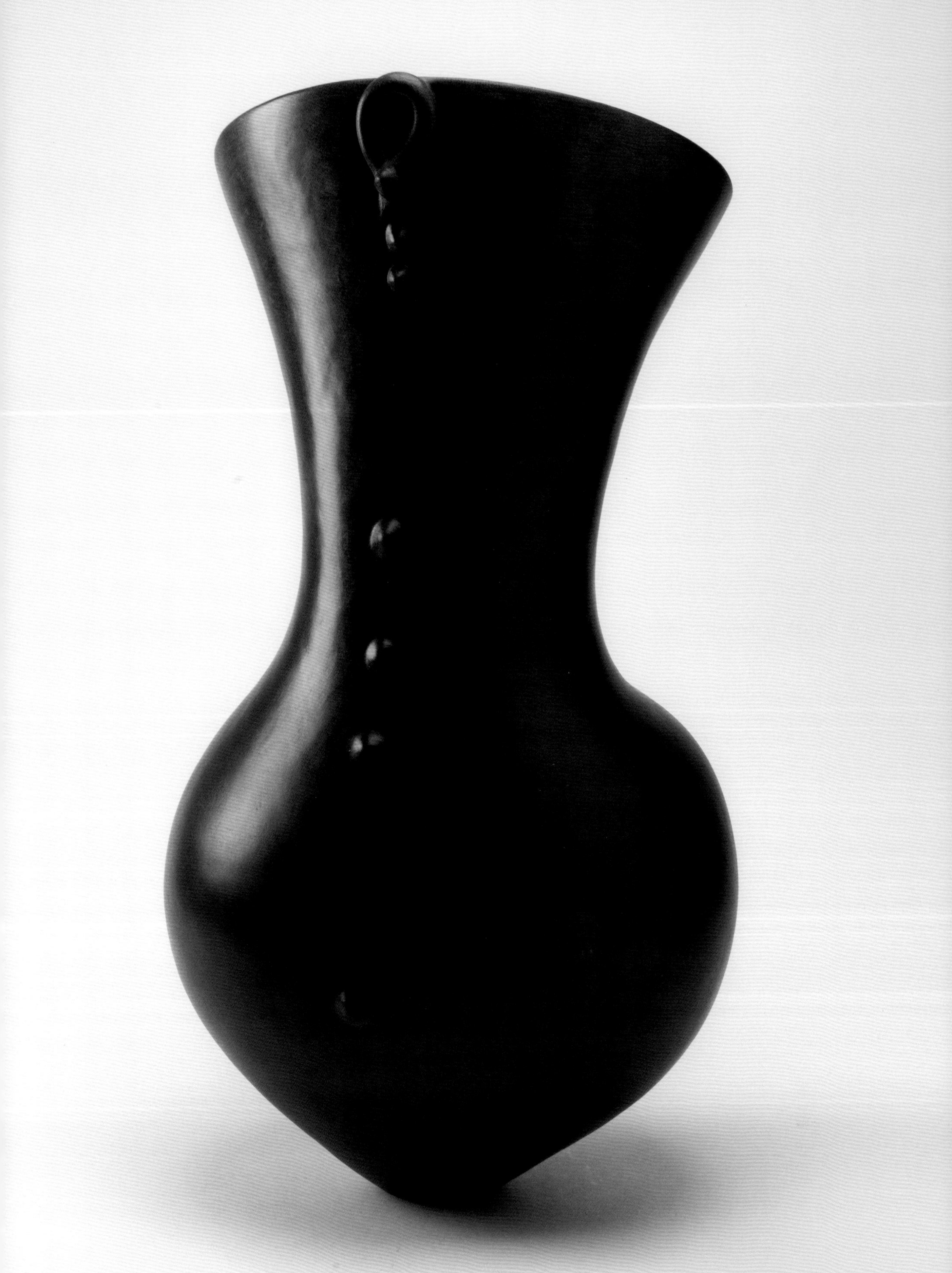

as well as things made from them like the decorated ostrich eggs used as water canteens in southern Africa (fig. 3). The spherical form echoes traditional earthen cooking vessels such as those found in her native Kenya, as well as water jars, beer pots, and numerous other utilitarian ceramics (fig. 4). A solitary protrusion calls to mind a belly button or nipple, while a column of similar nubs along the opposing side of the vessel evokes a spine or marks of scarification, enhancing the resonance with the human body (fig. 5). At the top of the spine is a ring, perhaps suggesting jewellery and other forms of bodily ornament. The flaring rim reinforces the language of ornament, referencing numerous traditions of headdress and coiffure, from the profiles of Mangbetu women of Central Africa (and the ceramic jugs depicting them) to the many other ways of crowning heads to mark status or enlightenment (fig. 6). The lustrous, variegated carbonized surface relates to Kerma ware of ancient Egypt and the black-on-black ceramics of Maria Martinez, as well as to other burnished-material surfaces such as carved wooden sculpture (fig. 7). Odundo's firing technique itself combines traditional and industrial approaches.[21]

Modern art and design enter Odundo's practice through both formal cues and symbolic meanings. The taut, organic profiles, pared-down surfaces, and abstracted figurative references all relate to modern sculpture by artists such as Brancusi, Hepworth,

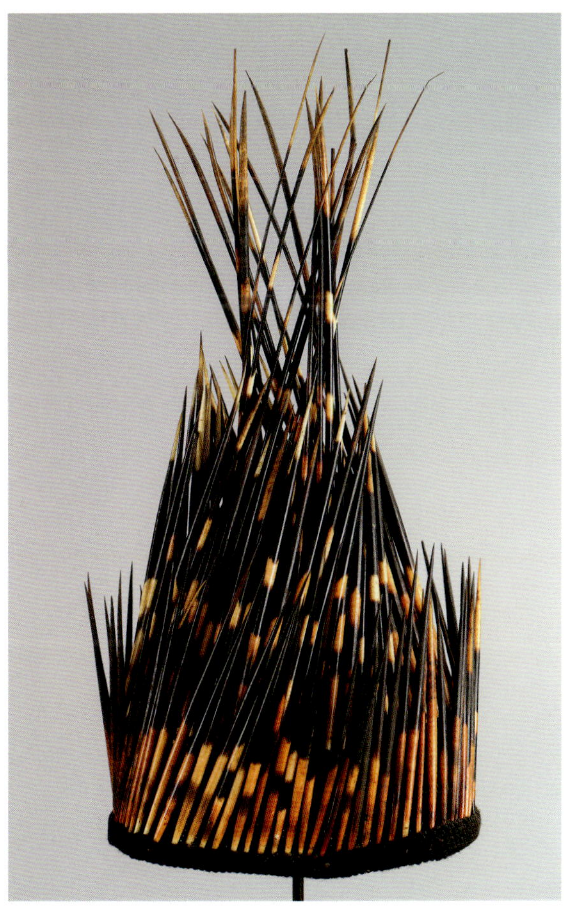

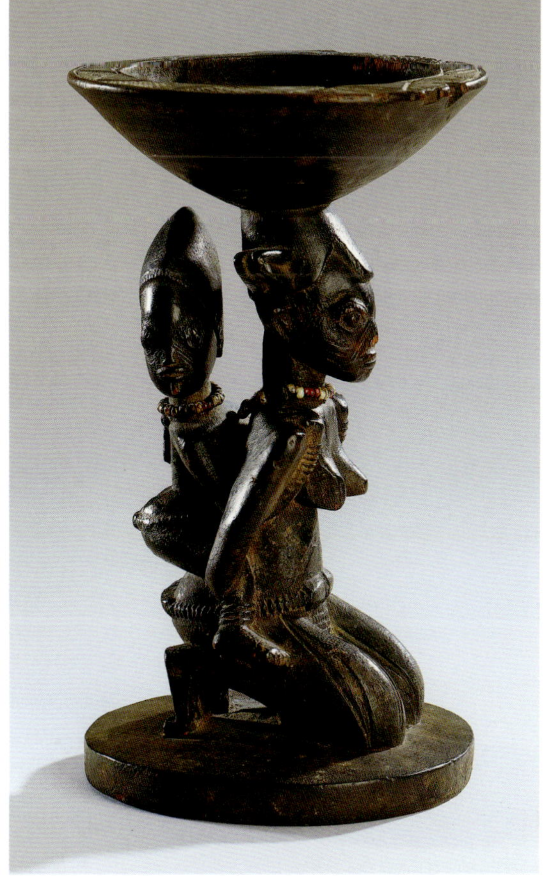

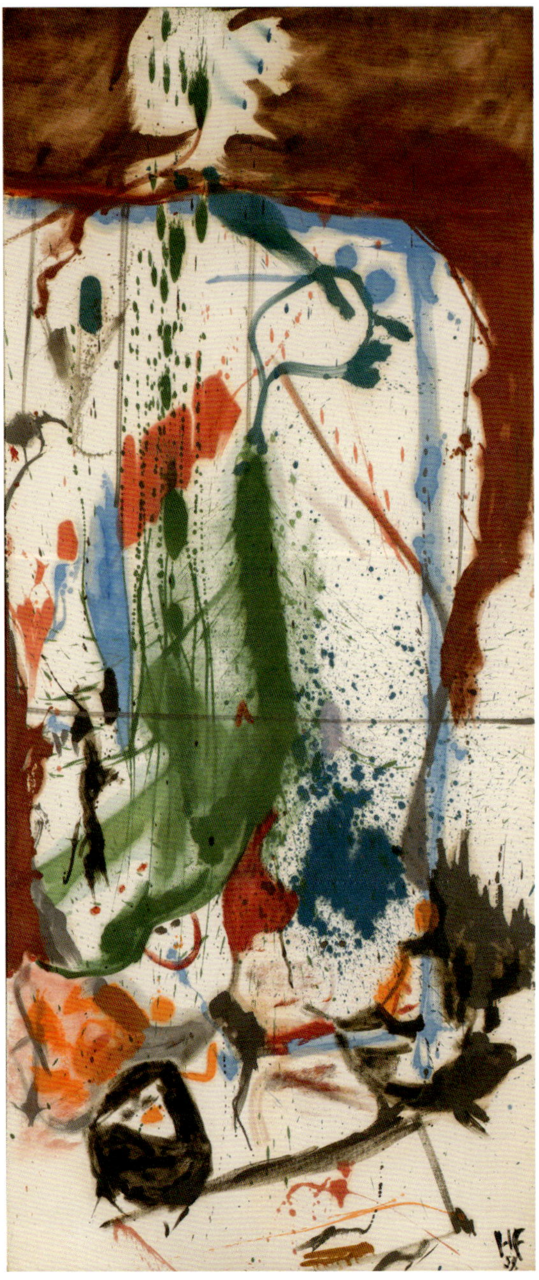

Fig. 8 Helen Frankenthaler, *Las Mayas*, 1958. Oil on canvas, 254 × 110 cm. Collection of Audrey and David Mirvish

Fig. 9 Magdalene Odundo, *Untitled*, 1994. Ceramic, 55 × 29 × 29 cm. Cooper Hewitt, Smithsonian Design Museum

and Moore, whose work she had first encountered at Kettle's Yard. Unlike these works, though, Odundo's sculptures are hollow vessels, reinforcing figurative references with feet, bellies, lips, and shoulders. Modern painting, too, has had an impact on Odundo's approach, most evident in the ways in which her profiles and transitions parallel gestural mark making. While her sense of gesture is more controlled, its extravagance, flair, and curvilinear qualities bring it into conversation with a work like *Las Mayas* (1958; fig. 8) by Helen Frankenthaler (1928–2011). Both *Las Mayas*, an abstracted reinterpretation of Francisco de Goya's *Majas on a Balcony*, and a work like Odundo's *Untitled* (1994 [Cooper Hewitt], fig. 9) embody figuration while continually skirting the outer edge

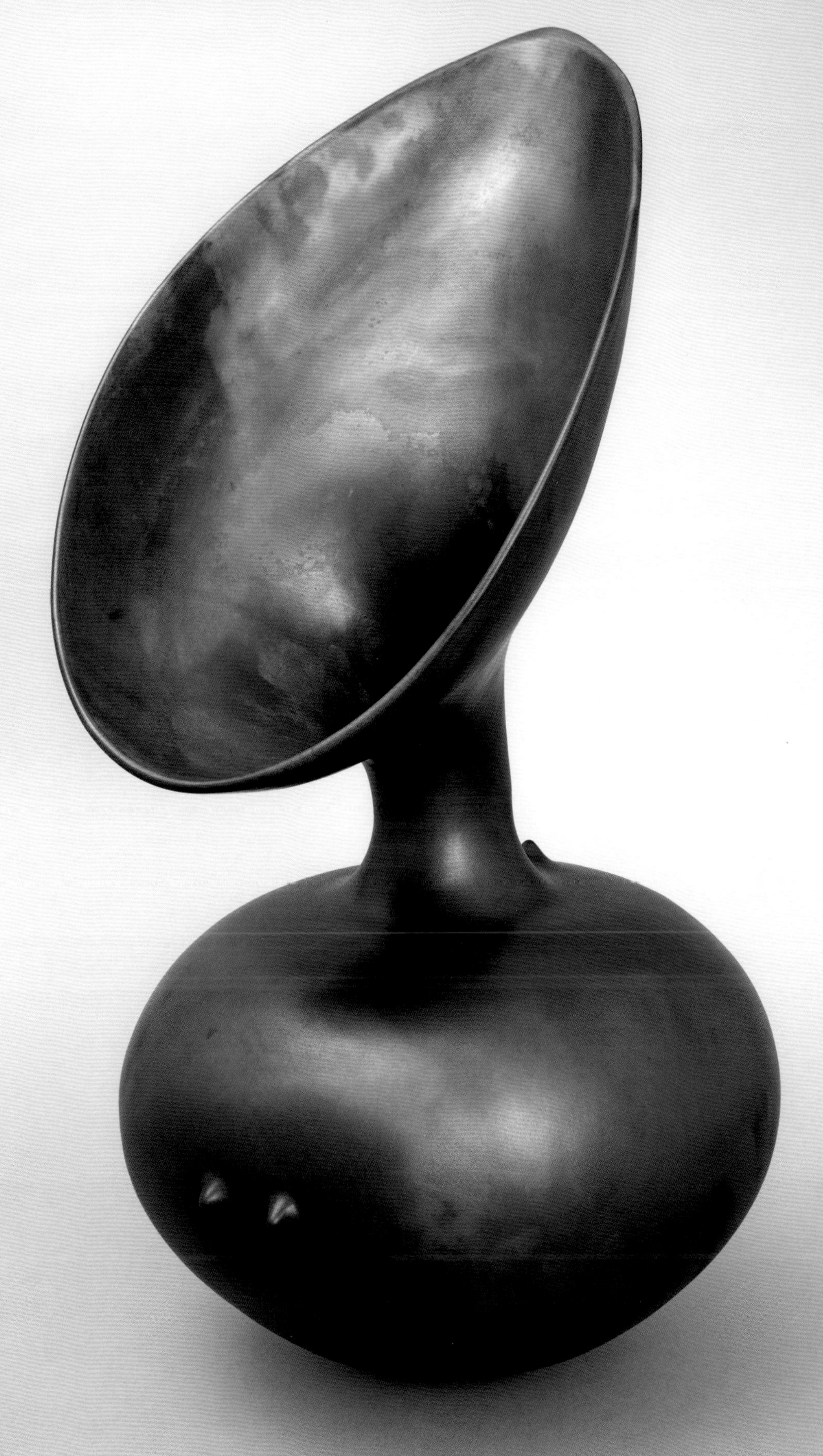

of human depiction. The painting and the vessel both express concentrated energy through curving lines and dramatic transitions between positive and negative spaces. Odundo's clearly articulated, interconnected volumes can also be understood in relation to the ordered proportions and conceptual framework of Josef Albers's (1888–1976) series of paintings and prints *Homage to the Square* (fig. 10). In all these works, abstract form, gesture, and geometry provoke association, reflection, and contemplation on the part of the viewer. Symbolic meanings are not explicitly stated, but rather co-constructed between artist and audience through a combination of individual and shared visual and cultural references.

Modern art, objects of world cultures, travel, and postcolonial political theory all had a significant impact on Odundo as a young artist in the 1970s. By the early 1980s, she began to synthesize these influences into a methodology of her own. An important influence on Odundo's practice of working transculturally was her mentor at London's Royal College of Art (RCA), Scottish artist and designer Eduardo Paolozzi (1924–2005). Odundo enrolled in the ceramics program at the RCA in 1979 after working for several years as a museum educator in London. She had hoped to study with Hans Coper, the influential German émigré potter who brought continental modernist design sensibilities to British studio ceramics, but he retired just before she arrived.[22] Paolozzi had joined the faculty as an influential graphic artist and sculptor, known widely for his work in collage and assemblage in what became British pop art of the 1950s and 1960s.[23] Paolozzi had long

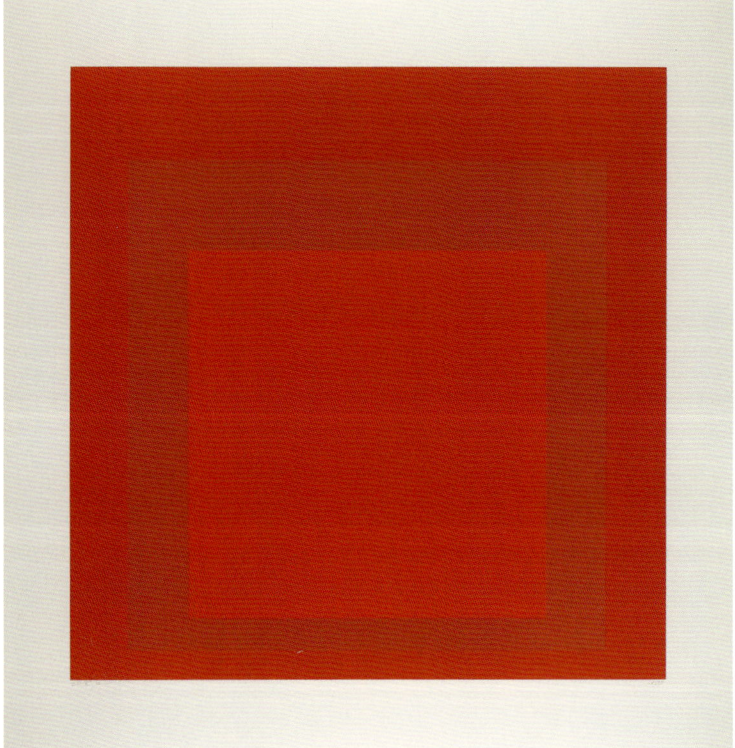

Fig. 10 Josef Albers, *Homage to the Square*, 1967. Screenprint on paper, 61.5 × 61.5 cm. Art Gallery of Ontario

visited ethnographic museums for inspiration and source material,[24] and he encouraged Odundo to visit the Museum of Mankind, a stand-alone institution for the Department of Ethnography of the British Museum.[25]

Like the Museum of Archaeology and Anthropology at Cambridge, the Museum of Mankind had assembled its collections specifically to gather and classify cultural belongings of non-Western people. The British Museum, founded in 1753, was a project of the Enlightenment, an age when rising European powers funded exploratory voyages to gather objects, specimens, and information about the world for both scientific and economic purposes. The resulting storehouses of artefacts and specimens cultivated the development of science as a discipline, while also establishing a dominant conceptual framework for structuring knowledge based on European supremacy. Such early museums worked in tandem with colonialism, plantation economies, and chattel slavery to create European power and cultural domination. Ethnographic collections facilitated the control of knowledge by British and other European powers to organize and define the world on their terms. Cambridge's Museum of Archaeology and Anthropology, founded in 1884 on collections gathered earlier in the nineteenth century, represents a Victorian iteration of the same ethos, albeit at a later stage of empire building. By the early 1980s, such ethnographic collections and the systems of knowledge and power that they represented were coming under increasing scrutiny with the growth of postcolonial scholarship. Writers such as Homi K. Bhabha, Stuart Hall, and Edward Said built on earlier scholarship to criticize the racist structures of Western power, which included its manifestation in institutions like ethnographic museums.

Just after Odundo was his student, Paolozzi began an exhibition project at the Museum of Mankind in 1985 that would embody the problematic issues of working with ethnographic collections. Titled *Lost Magic Kingdoms*, the resulting exhibition was important for beginning to move away from the discourses of "primitivism" and "primitive art," which were still in wide circulation.[26] The project sought to elevate appreciation of the artefacts by recontextualizing them to offer new meanings, while emphasizing their inherent power and ambiguity rather than foregrounding questions of cultural authenticity. The project also stands as one of the earliest interventions into a museum collection by a contemporary artist, a format that has since become an essential tool for museums to animate ethnographic and historical collections for current audiences. For artists, such projects offer new avenues for institutional engagement, while also grounding their work in (and often revising) art historical narratives.

Yet *Lost Magic Kingdoms* also reinforced biases embedded in Western perspectives on non-Western objects. The title characterizes Indigenous cultures as existing only in the past, as well as their status as exotic or "magical" to the West. Paolozzi's disinterest in the original context of the artefacts, even what cultures they were from, exemplifies how Western artists and institutions continued to feel a sense of entitlement to exploit such works for their own purposes.[27] The exhibition also included numerous funerary and ritual items, including human remains almost certainly collected without permission. As a methodology for working transculturally, the project is illustrative of its moment: critical of earlier discourses of primitivism while still embodying racist Western cultural hierarchies.

By contrast, Odundo's approach to working with ethnographic and historical collections both as an artist and as a curator is synthetic rather than extractive. She draws from global cultures yet does not make distinctions between Western and non-Western, art and artefact, thereby helping to dismantle lingering hierarchies of cultural value. She disregards temporal distinctions, giving precedence to neither the contemporary nor the ancient and thereby avoiding discourses of authenticity, exoticism, and nostalgia. Her deep knowledge about many of the works she draws from, particularly among ceramics from various communities in Africa, enables her to read objects, perceiving some of their original meanings and connecting to their symbolic value. Even with works she knows very little about, she approaches them with respect for their original context and purpose. She does not aim to give these objects new meanings but rather responds to them, whether historical or contemporary, for how they point to our shared humanity, identifying commonalities such as the ways objects signal moments in the life cycle, how materials receive careful attention to their physical properties, and how subtle transitions allude to parts of our bodies. She then synthesizes these attributes into a formal language that is uniquely her own, rendering the initial inspiration a faint echo. By emphasizing underlying attributes, shared cultural forms, and synthesis, Odundo avoids pitfalls of appropriation and other culturally extractive methods.

In her curatorial practice, Odundo similarly approaches projects intuitively in relation to her primary work as an artist. While Odundo had engaged with collections as source material for many years, her first museum intervention that could be considered curatorial was *Acknowledged Sources* at the Russell-Coates Art Gallery and Museum in Bournemouth in 2002 (fig. 11). In this project, Odundo presented her work within the context of a historic house, using the opportunity, as Simon Olding describes, "to embark on the installation (an entirely new approach in her career) within the template of her own more regular use of museums as a starting point for acquiring knowledge."[28] More recently, she has participated curatorially in a number of projects where her work was on view alongside historical and contemporary objects, including *The Journey of Things* in 2019 and *Magdalene Odundo in Cambridge* in 2021–2022.[29] In each of these projects, Odundo made explicit the connections between her work and her sources of inspiration, allowing viewers to understand more clearly her process of synthesis. The present publication appears on the occasion of Odundo's first exhibition in Canada, *Magdalene*

Odundo: A Dialogue with Objects, which similarly includes her works in conversation with both historical and contemporary artworks and artefacts. In this case, Odundo selected works on the basis of long-standing affinity, for example pieces by Ladi Kwali (see fig. 2) and ceramic objects from her native Kenya, as well as works new to her, such as a painting by Canadian artist Denyse Thomasos (fig. 12). Through these and other choices, Odundo demonstrates her practice of relation, wherein she enters into an equal dialogue with works from a range of cultures to uncover connections and correspondences. In this way, her curatorial work emerges from and in tandem with her studio practice, together representing a forward-looking approach to working transculturally with colonial collections.

Changing discourses around the colonial collecting histories of museums are revealing the broader implications of this aspect of Odundo's practice. Since the early 1980s, when she developed her methodology, critiques of Western institutional collections have steadily increased in nuance and ambition. Key artist interventions by Fred Wilson, James Luna, and others beginning in the late 1980s have highlighted structural and representational imbalances of power.[30] Questions surrounding colonial-era collection gathering and repatriation have come to dominate conversations concerning the practices of ethnographic, encyclopaedic, and world culture museums in Europe's former colonial powers. France, Germany, and other nations are reevaluating repatriation laws, with restitution of the Benin bronzes becoming perhaps the marquee example.[31] Shifting norms for the storage, display, and repatriation of Indigenous funerary belongings and human remains

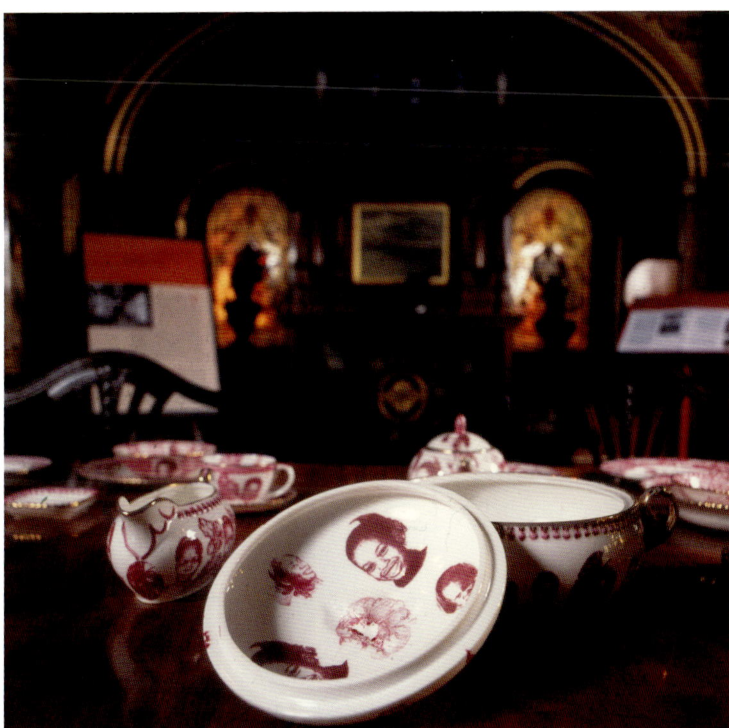

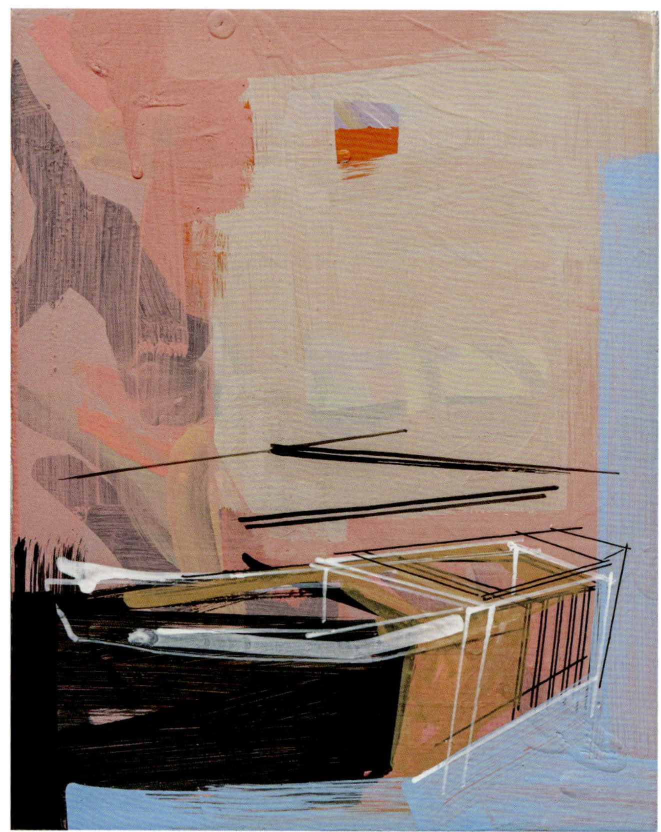

Fig. 12 Denyse Thomasos, *Untitled*, 2012. Acrylic on canvas, 26.4 × 21 cm. Dr. Kenneth Montague | The Wedge Collection

have led to numerous returns while also cultivating greater consultation between institutions and Indigenous communities.[32] The British Museum in London and the Museum of Archaeology and Anthropology at Cambridge, among others, have begun to reckon with their colonial roots, particularly their ties to the slave trade, while facing regular calls for restitution that challenge their institutional model.

With the imbalances of wealth and power that enabled the growth of Western museum collections more visible now than ever before, Odundo's practice stands as newly relevant. In generating connections across diverse cultural traditions without asserting hegemonic structures or prioritizing European traditions, she de-centers Western hierarchies and epistemologies by using the very institutions built to maintain them, while modelling a vision that centers equity, agency, and cultural connectivity. The political dimension of Odundo's engagement with colonial museum collections to support an anti-colonial practice, though less considered in discussions of her work than the cultural synthesis it embodies, was explicitly addressed in the 1992 exhibition *Columbus Drowning* at the Rochdale Art Gallery (now Touchstones Rochdale) in Greater Manchester county.[33] Organized by Scottish-Ghanaian artist Maud Sulter, the show included works by Odundo and others visualizing "the ancestral connection between our diasporan heritage, in West Africa, the Caribbean and the Americas, that bring us back in touch with our own forebearers."[34] That type of critical examination of diasporic heritage had precedents in the Black arts movement that emerged in the UK in the 1980s. The movement was made up of Black diasporic artists and thinkers, with roots in both the Caribbean and Africa, who questioned and critiqued racist social structures steeped in colonialism. Buoyed by the expansion of postcolonial theory within cultural studies, literature, and art history, artists and filmmakers including Sonia Boyce, Rotimi Fani-Kayode, Isaac Julien, Keith Piper, and Yinka Shonibare explored Black, diasporic, and queer British identities and experiences, exhibiting their works in both mainstream and dedicated spaces.[35] Integral to their work was an exploration of identity as contingent and continually shifting, a "historically constructed semiotic field" resisting notions of authenticity and essentialism.[36] In representing contingent Black diasporic identities, they also shared what Kobena Mercer describes as a "quest to confront past trauma by bringing its violence into the field of representation for the first time."[37] While the imagery used by these artists was at times ambiguous, the core concerns of Black identity within a British context in the wake of colonialism were clearly legible in the use of figures, text, repeating patterns, and, often, film-based media. As diaspora theory gained

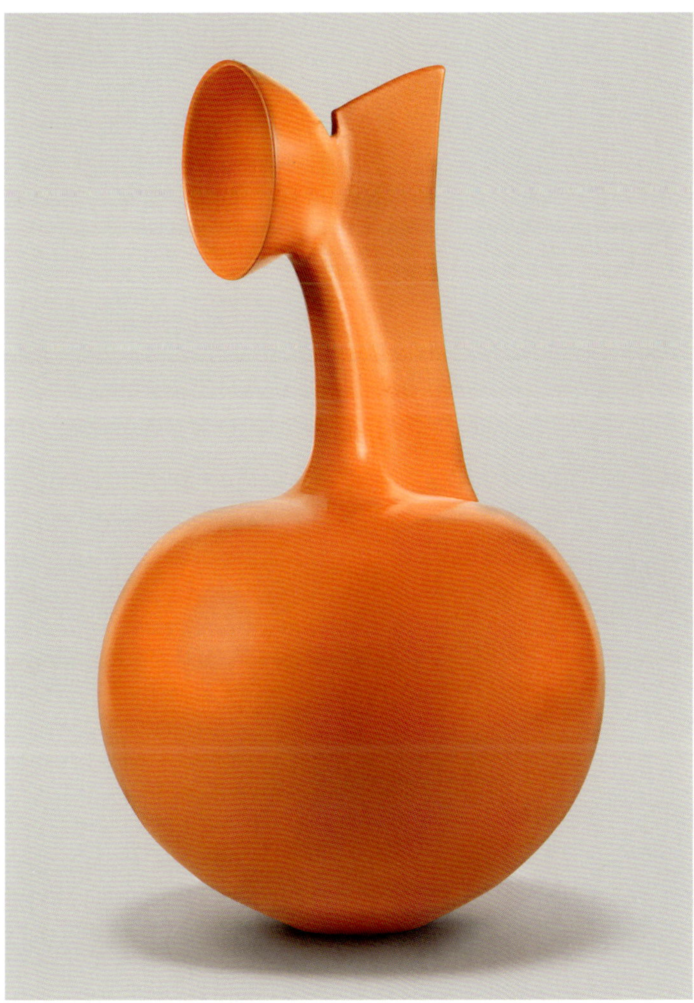

Fig. 31 (Alternate view) Magdalene Odundo, *Untitled*, 1987. Ceramic, 37 × 22 × 22 cm. Maxine and Stuart Frankel Foundation for Art

ground in the 1990s and 2000s, the specifically British postcolonial context broadened to include other geographies such as the Caribbean, Brazil, and the United States.[38]

While Odundo engaged with current social issues, the political dimensions of her work were largely illegible within the discourses of the Black arts movement.[39] She explored themes of identity and diaspora in her artwork in ways that many other artists and viewers simply did not perceive. The forms, while evocative and perhaps visibly "African," are also evasive, in that they do not connect to any one specific tradition. Viewers typically associate the vessels with symbolic meanings rather than with conceptual or political sub-texts.[40] Their beauty and exquisite rendering also foreground skill, labour, and material sensibilities, ideas that were less widespread among Black diasporic artists in the late twentieth century. Whereas most artists associated with the Black arts movement used graphic, image, and text-based strategies to position their work in relation to a specific political moment, Odundo expressed her politics through a material approach informed by historical sources and sparing in contemporary reference points. Like the apprenticeship model of education, Odundo's work demonstrates rather than explains, embodying her principles of non-extractive transcultural inspiration rather than foregrounding those ideas as the explicit thematic content of the work.

The largely illegible ways in which Odundo's work participates in postcolonial discourses derive also from her use of silence and opacity. Silence in Odundo's work can include the absence of explicit imagery or her reticence, until recently, in naming its relationship to colonialism. Yet the most significant manifestation of silence in her work takes shape in the interiors of the forms. For Odundo, interiors are critical in creating the void that is at the centre of all her ceramics. These interiors are accessible to varying degrees, yet we often perceive the inside of the object through its exterior shape. Philosopher Martin Heidegger proposed that the central void of a pottery vessel was in fact the thing, with the ceramic wall merely describing its limit.[41] In a similar way, Odundo's ceramics, while extravagant on the outside, also hold a very particular kind of void on the inside.

Her internal voids create spaces for silence. Observing her work closely, slowing down to perceive its nuances and envisioning the interior, we can depart from the noise of daily life to enter a space of quietude and reflection. The references to ritual objects enumerated above can retreat to the subconscious level, while we speculatively imagine the internal space of the particular work we are taking in. This contained silence becomes a conduit for contemplation, where each of us encounters our own questions, concerns, or troubles. For Odundo, the silence allows her to come to terms with the violence of growing up in a colonial society.[42] In lectures she has often included an image of colonial soldiers in Kenya, yet she has chosen not to speak at length about these experiences or themes directly in relation to her art. The silence she creates in her work has extended to her public reticence in discussing it in this way.

Odundo's use of silence can be understood within the theoretical framework of opacity as proposed by Caribbean philosopher and poet Édouard Glissant. For Glissant, "the right to opacity" was the power to remain ambiguous, unintelligible, or not fully understood.[43] Its opposite was transparency, which he understood as a Western effort towards conformity and uniformity of value and meaning. With opacity, we co-exist in our mutual unknowability as individuals and societies, respecting diverse visions of humanity that run counter to cultural hierarchies and the dominance of Western epistemologies. Opacity is a foundational aspect of *relation*, Glissant's theory of non-hierarchical cultural interaction and exchange.[44]

In the context of Odundo's work, opacity operates in several ways. It can be the unknowability of the interiors of her forms: a space partially grasped, but not fully seen or experienced. The works are opaque ceramic, concealing the real or imagined contents of the interior. The limited way in which Odundo addresses or reveals their postcolonial aspect embodies opacity. The refinement and elegance render opaque the violence held within them. The absence of imagery makes them act as reflections of our imagination. They are opaque even in their sources, denying us the clarity of a precise point of origin. Through these myriad forms of opacity, Odundo preserves a certain reverence for the interior silence she creates, refusing to let her work be fully perceptible. She also resists the colonial epistemic system in which she was raised, projecting instead one of relation, in Glissant's sense. She extends this opacity when she works transculturally In responding to objects from other cultures, acknowledging the impossibility of their full comprehension. Within her methodology of working across cultures in relation, she preserves her own agency as both a holder and a creator of culture.

Alongside the growth of postcolonial and diasporic scholarship, developments in the art world over the last ten or so years have expanded the readable meanings in Odundo's work. Ceramics has moved from the margins to the mainstream, with a corresponding rise in the visual literacy of the medium among contemporary art audiences. Similarly, as Elizabeth Harney considers elsewhere in this volume, contemporary African and African diasporic art has become much more widespread in Western art centers. Perhaps most compellingly, recent developments in Black feminist thought has helped to expand the theoretical frameworks for analyzing cultural discourses initiated and maintained by Black women. Authors like Tina Campt, Saidiya Hartman, Christina Sharpe, and others reveal ways in which Black women artists and thinkers continue to offer new ways of understanding the past as well as possibilities for the future. Seen in this context, Odundo's work exemplifies anti-colonial practice by resisting hierarchies and imperatives, and participating in discourses of opacity, invisibility, and silence that have been central in theorizing Black diasporic life. With new layers of meaning still being revealed, Odundo's work begins to speak anew to generations of viewers.

Notes

1. The first exhibition to show Odundo's work alongside historical objects was *Resonance and Inspiration: New Works by Magdalene Odundo* (2006) at the Harn Museum of Art, Gainesville, Florida, curated by Susan Cooksey. *Magdalene Odundo: A Dialogue with Objects* (2023–2024) at the Gardiner Museum, Toronto, is the occasion that prompts the present publication. Later projects include *The Journey of Things* (2019) at the Hepworth Wakefield, Wakefield, England, and Sainsbury Centre, Norwich, England, and *Odundo in Cambridge* (2021–2022) at the Fitzwilliam Museum, Cambridge, England.

2. Odundo had been exposed to African objects, as well as those from other cultures, in museum collections prior to moving to England, for example at the Kenya National Museum in Nairobi.

3. Emmanuel Cooper, "The Clay of Life: The Ceramic Vessels of Magdalene Odundo," in *Magdalene Odundo*, ed. Anthony Slayter-Ralph (Aldershot, Hampshire, UK: Lund Humphries, 2004), 9. Odundo had an early patron, Isabel Beverly, an English woman living in Kenya, who facilitated her study abroad in England.

4. Andrew Bonacina, "Magdalene Odundo: The Journey of Things," in Magdalene Odundo et al., *The Journey of Things* (London: In Other Words, 2019), n.p.

5. Magdalene Odundo, conversation with the author, June 28, 2023.

6. Bonacina, "Magdalene Odundo," n.p.

7. In Kenya, the British colonial government designated ancestral or tribal areas and villages as reserves, a term whose meanings differed depending on context.

8. Odundo, conversation with the author, June 28, 2023.

9. W. E. B. Du Bois, *The Souls of Black Folk: Essays and Sketches* (Chicago: A. C. McClurg & Co., 1903).

10. Franz Fanon, *Black Skin, White Masks*, trans. Charles L. Markmann (New York: Grove Press, 1967).

11. University of Cambridge, "About the Centre," accessed August 23, 2023, https://www.african.cam.ac.uk/about.

12. Monique Kerman, *Contemporary British Artists of African Descent and the Unburdening of a Generation* (Cham, Switzerland: Palgrave Macmillan by Springer Nature, 2017), 29; Odundo, conversation with the author, June 29 and July 7, 2023.

13. Odundo taught at University of Creative Arts from 2001 until 2014. She has served as chancellor since 2019.

14. See Emmanuel Cooper, *Bernard Leach: Life and Work* (New Haven: Published for the Paul Mellon Centre for Studies in British Art by Yale University Press, 2003), and Bernard Leach, *A Potter's Book* (London: Faber and Faber, 1940).

15. For a critical account of Leach, see Edmund De Waal, *Bernard Leach* (London: Tate Gallery Publishing, 1998).

16. For a full account of the Abuja Pottery Training Centre, see Tanya Harrod, *The Last Sane Man: Michael Cardew: Modern Pots, Colonialism, and the Counterculture* (New Haven: Published for the Paul Mellon Centre for Studies in British Art by Yale University Press, 2012).

17. While on this trip, Odundo also went to Ghana and other parts of Nigeria, visiting friends she had made at the Centre of African Studies in Cambridge, which speaks to her participation in broader diasporic networks. Cooper, "The Clay of Life," 15.

18. Elsbeth Joyce Court, "Magdalene A. N. Odundo: Pathways to Path Maker, *Critical Interventions* 11, no. 1 (2017): 81. Kwali had visited the West Surrey College of Art and Design in 1960 at the invitation of Henry Hammond, the leader of the ceramics program there. Sophie Heath, *Henry Hammond* (Farnham, UK: Craft Study Centre, 2006), 10. Kwali later had several influential workshop and exhibition tours in the UK and United States.

19. Odundo, conversation with the author, July 7, 2023.

20. Bonacina, "Magdalene Odundo," n.p.; Kerman, *Contemporary British Artists*, 34.

21. The carbonization comes from burning organic materials much like in a traditional pit firing, a technique practiced globally, but done so in a container inside a kiln called a saggar. Odundo first encountered the approach in the pottery factories of England's ceramic industry in Stoke-on-Trent. Kerman, *Contemporary British Artists*, 39.

22. Cooper, "The Clay of Life," 24.

23. Paolozzi was a founder of the Independent Group in 1952 and widely celebrated for his irreverence and influence on British pop art. See Daniel F. Herrmann, ed., *Eduardo Paolozzi* (London: Whitechapel Gallery, 2017).

24. Eduardo Paolozzi, "Primitive Art, Paris and London," in Eduardo Paolozzi, *Lost Magic Kingdoms and Six Paper Moons from Nahuatl: An Exhibition at the Museum of Mankind* (London: British Museum Publications, 1985), 9. Pablo Picasso, André Breton, and other continental artists famously visited anthropology museums and curio stores, where they were inspired by objects from non-Western cultures. The practice was not widespread in the UK at the time Paolozzi began doing it in the 1940s.

25. Tania Moore, "Artists, Institutions and Objects: Magdalene Odundo as Artist-Curator," in Odundo et al., *The Journey of Things*, n.p. The Museum of Mankind was active from 1970 until 1999, when it was reintegrated with the main collections at the British Museum.

26. See Malcolm McLeod, "Paolozzi, Surrealism, Ethnography," in Paolozzi, *Lost Magic Kingdoms*, 14–58. The year before this project, the Museum of Modern Art in New York sparked vigorous debate about the concept of and use of the term "primitive art" with their exhibition *Primitivism*. See William Rubin, ed., *Primitivism in 20th Century Art: Affinity of the Tribal and the Modern* (New York: Museum of Modern Art, 1984).

27. McLeod, "Paolozzi, Surrealism, Ethnography," 38; Tania Moore, "Artists, Institutions and Objects," n.p.

28. Simon Olding, "Ceramics and Curatorship," in *Magdalene Odundo*, ed. Anthony Slayter-Ralph (Aldershot, Hampshire: Lund Humphries, 2004), 84.

29. *Magdalene Odundo: The Journey of Things*, The Hepworth Wakefield, February 16–June 2, 2019, and Sainsbury Centre, Norwich, August 3–December 15, 2019. *Magdalene Odundo in Cambridge*, Fitzwilliam Museum, October 5, 2021– July 24, 2022.

30. Indigenous artist James Luna became well known for his *Artifact Piece* (1987), a performance in which he occupied a display case at the Museum of Man (now the Museum of Us) in San Diego, while Fred Wilson gained wide acclaim

for *Mining the Museum* (1992), in which he included objects associated with slavery and the slave trade in an installation at the Maryland Historical Society. See Laura M. Evans, "The Artifact Piece Revisited," in Nancy J. Bloomberg, ed., *Action and Agency: Advancing the Dialogue on Native Performance Art* (Denver: Denver Art Museum, 2010), and Fred Wilson, *Mining the Museum: An Installation* (Baltimore: Contemporary, 1994).

31. See Alex Marshall, "Art Restitution Gets a Curveball," *New York Times*, June 6, 2023.

32. In the United States, the Native American Graves Protection and Repatriation Act (NAGPRA) passed in 1990, significantly shifting norms for the collection and display of Indigenous funerary objects and human remains. Institutions like the Museum of Anthropology at the University of British Columbia in Vancouver have similarly developed significant relationships with Indigenous communities, exploring new models of ownership, access, and community engagement; see https://moa.ubc.ca/indigenous-access-and-engagement/.

33. *The Journey of Things* and *Magdalene Odundo in Cambridge* carefully considered the artist's relationship to myriad cultures, but neither approached this aspect of her work as political or anti-colonial.

34. Maud Sulter, *Columbus Drowning* (Rochdale, UK: The Gallery, 1992), 30. Other exhibitions at the time, including *Africa Explores* (1991) at the Museum for African Art in New York and *Africa95* (1995), a Britain-wide series of exhibitions and events, engaged with the politics of contemporary African art, yet did not address Odundo or her practice specifically as anti-colonial.

35. See Kobena Mercer, *Travel & See: Black Diaspora Art Practices since the 1980s* (Durham, NC: Duke University Press, 2016).

36. Mercer, *Travel & See*, 29.

37. Mercer, 277.

38. See Paul Gilroy, *The Black Atlantic: Modernity and Double Consciousness* (London: Verso, 1993).

39. Odundo, conversation with the author, August 28, 2023.

40. Object types such as vessels, furniture, and clothing have histories in the West linked with craft, material culture, and the decorative arts more so than with painting and sculpture. In these histories, meanings typically emerge through objects embodying cultural expression rather than explicitly thematizing content. Recent significant work to restore the conceptual underpinnings of vessels includes Christina Sharpe, "What Could a Vessel Be?," in *The Milk of Dreams*, ed. Manuela Hansen (Venice: La Biennale di Venezia, 2022), 367–73.

41. Martin Heidegger and Eugene T. Gendlin, *What Is a Thing*, trans. W. B. Barton and Vera Deutsch (Chicago: Henry Regnery, 1967); originally published as "Das Ding," in *Einblick in das was ist* (Freiburg: Bremer Vorträge, 1949).

42. Odundo, conversation with the author, May 24, 2023.

43. Édouard Glissant, "For Opacity," in *Poetics of Relation*, trans. Betsy Wing (Ann Arbor: University of Michigan Press, 1997); see also John E. Drabinski and Marisa Parham, *Theorizing Glissant: Sites and Citations Creolizing the Canon* (London: Rowman & Littlefield International, 2015).

44. Other theories of Black visibility can be productively brought into conversation with Odundo's work, including Ralph Ellison's theory of invisibility (see Ellison, *Invisible Man* [New York: Random House, 1952]), and Fred Moten's notion of blur, a shifting, imprecise, and not fully knowable theory of Blackness (see Moten, *Black and Blur* [Durham, NC: Duke University Press, 2017]). Silence, adjacent to invisibility, as an active strategy for self-preservation also appears as a theme in works by Saidiya Hartman (see Hartman, *Lose Your Mother* [New York: Macmillan Publishers, 2008]), and Tina Campt (see Campt, "Quiet Soundings: The Grammar of Black Futurity," in *Listening to Images* [Durham, NC: Duke University Press, 2017]), and is the subject of increasing scholarly inquiry (see, for example, Luisa Santos, ed., *Cultures of Silence: The Power of Untold Narratives* [New York: Routledge, 2022]).

Fig. 13 Magdalene Odundo, *Untitled*,
1988. Ceramic, 39 × 23.8 × 23.8 cm.
Maxine and Stuart Frankel Foundation
for Art

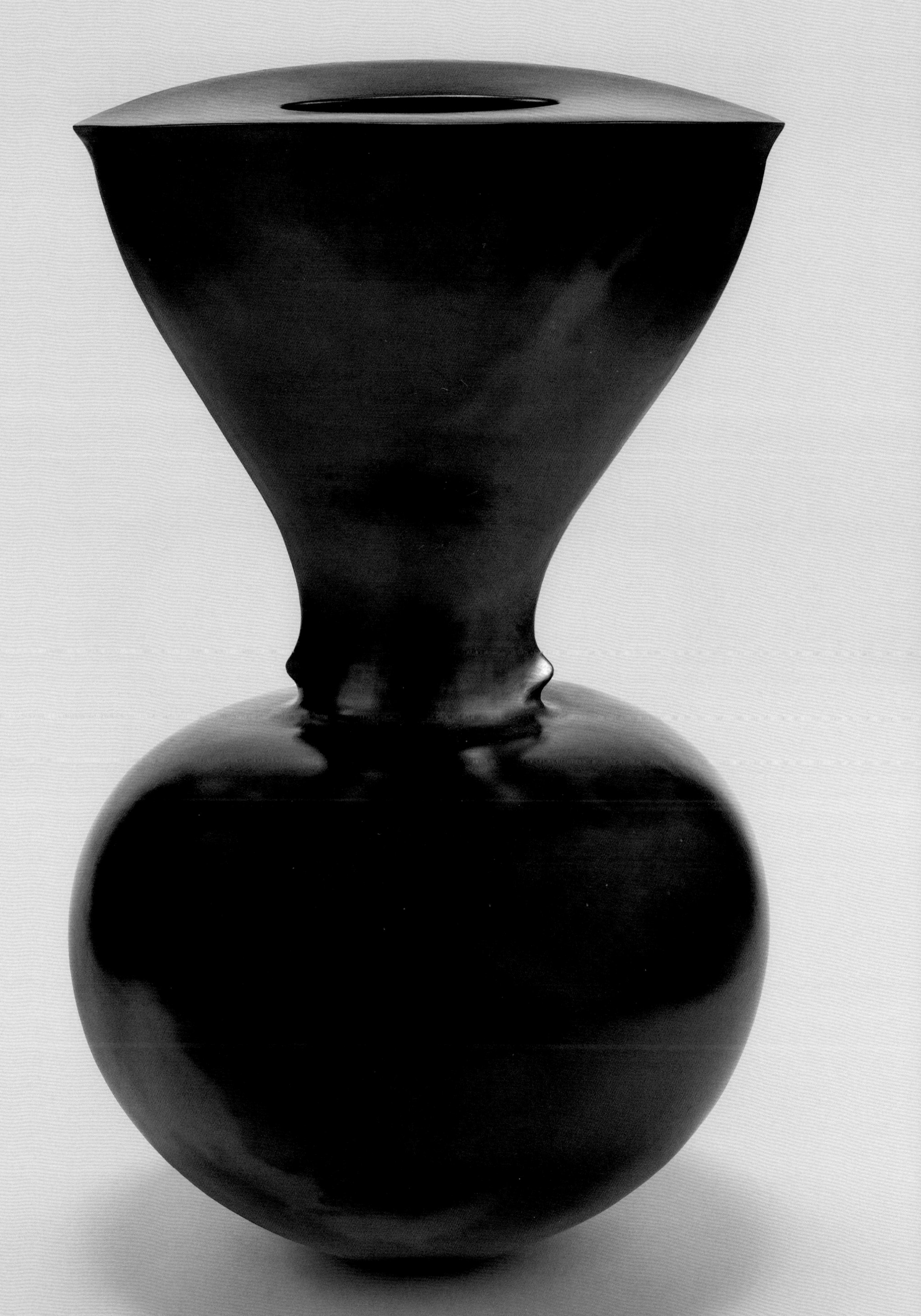

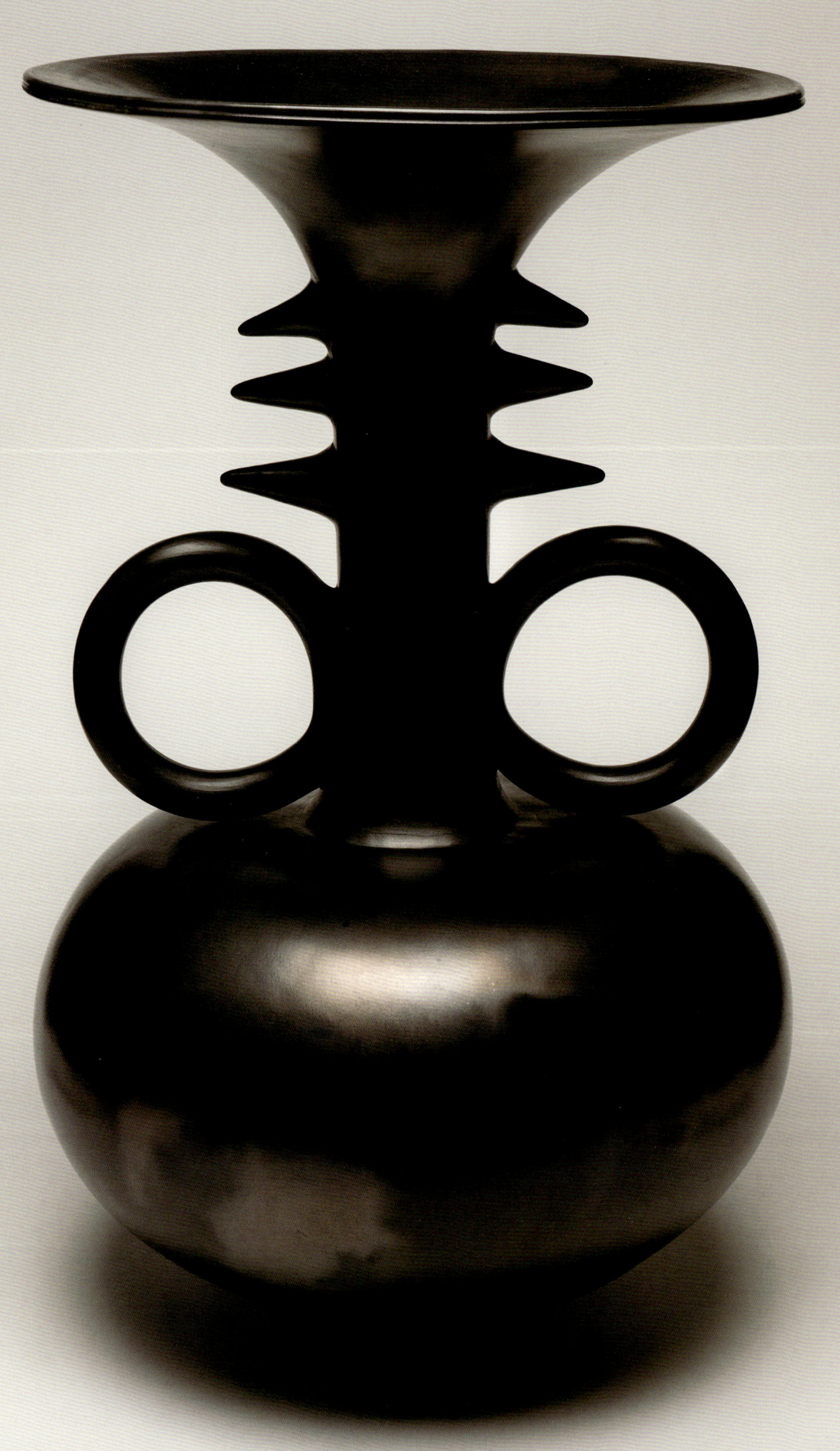

Fig. 14 Magdalene Odundo, *Untitled*, 1990. Ceramic, 40.6 × 25.4 × 25.4 cm. Brooklyn Museum

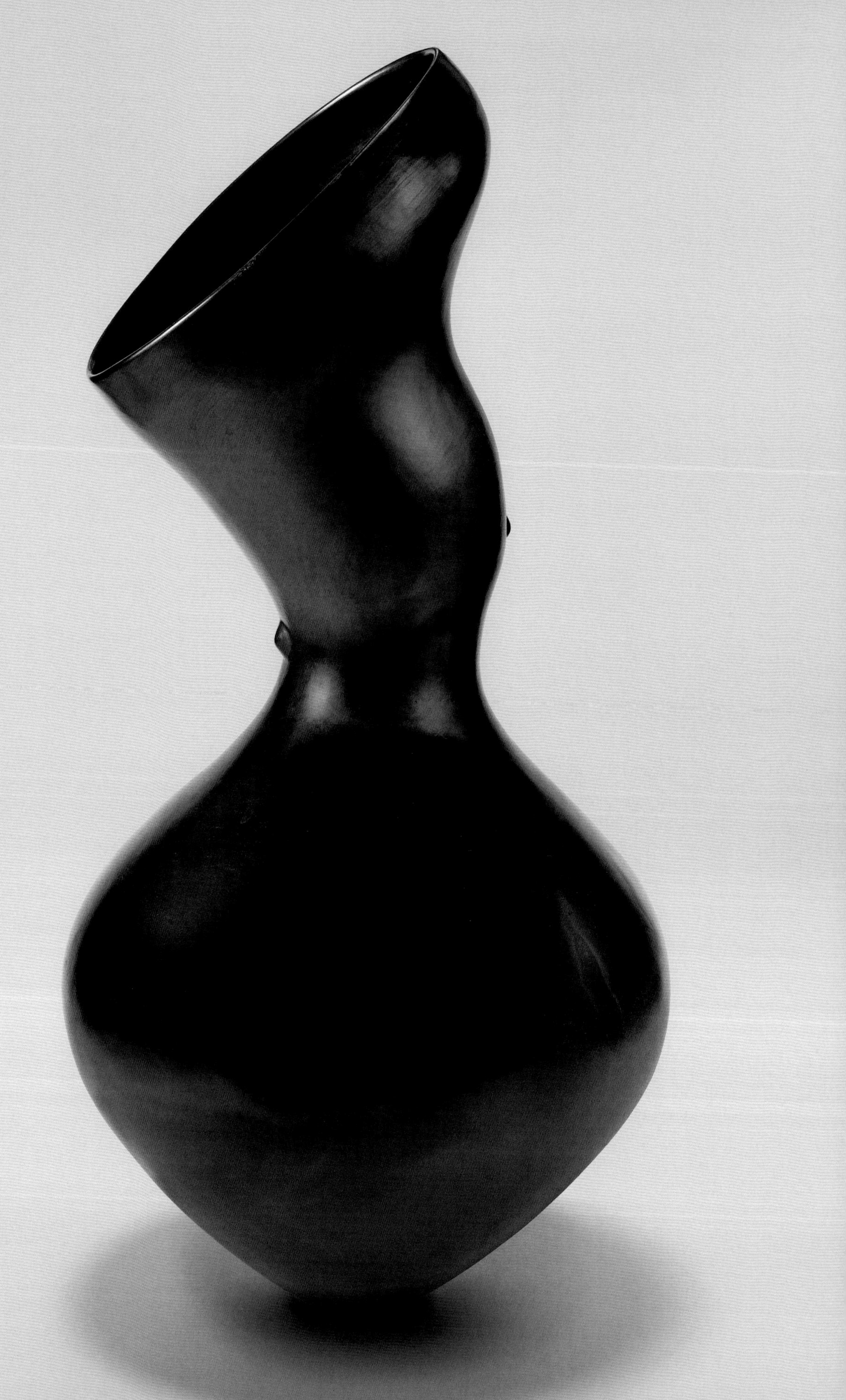

Fig. 15 Magdalene Odundo, *Untitled*,
2005–2006. Ceramic, 56.5 × 29 × 29 cm.
Maxine and Stuart Frankel Foundation
for Art

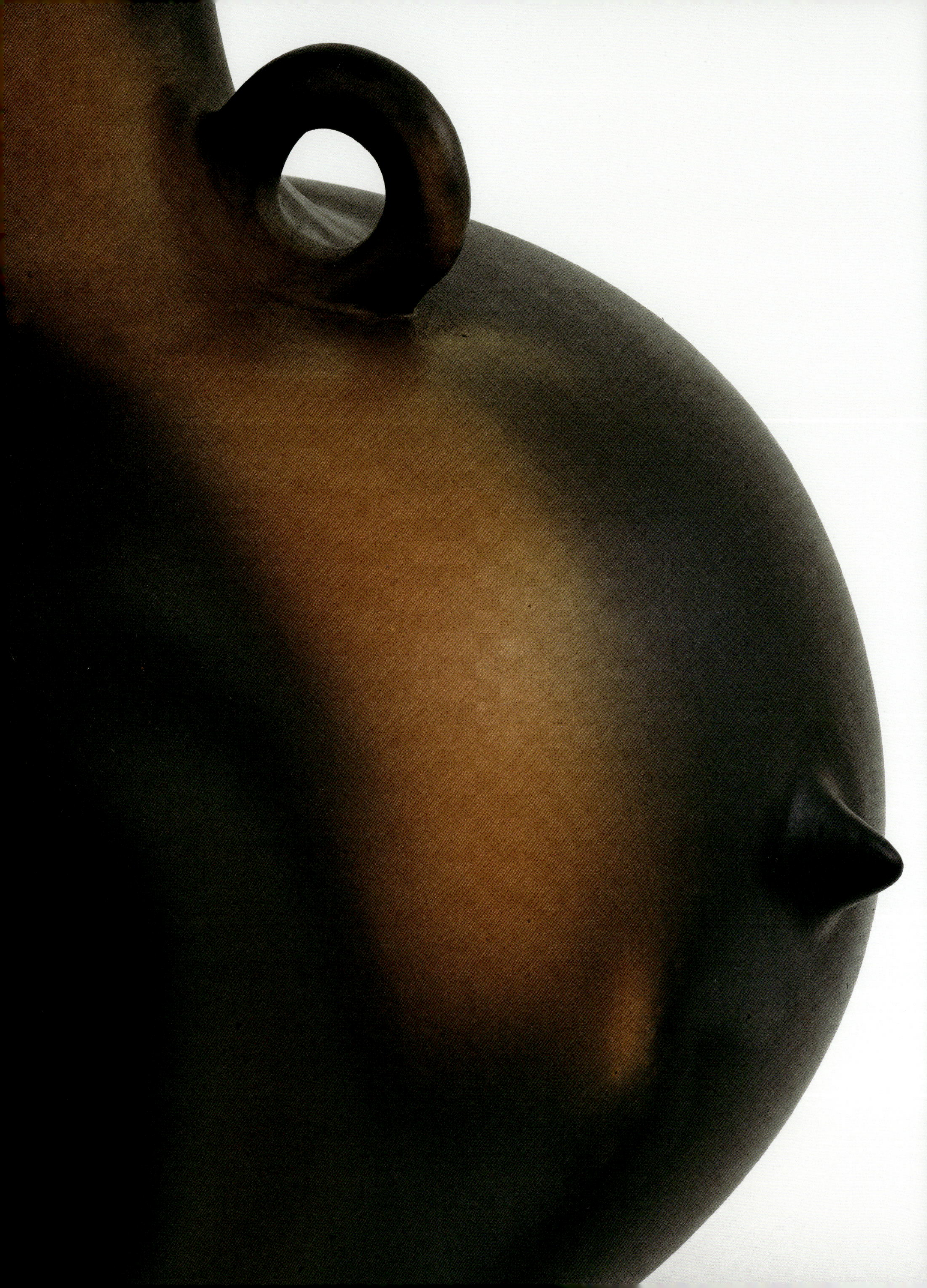

Barbara Thompson

Magdalene Odundo's Return to "That Chance Dance with the Fire"

A ceramic artist promptly learns that each kiln is a beast in its own right, with mechanical particularities and quirks that need coaxing, beguiling, and manipulating to optimize the chemistry between the artist, clay, oxygen, fuel, and fire. The artist's navigational bond with the volatility of each firing can determine the success or failure of a piece and its power to reflect the artistic intention. Magdalene Odundo has perfected the balance between human will and the quantum mechanics of the kiln, and, like dancing a tango, this relationship is filled with dynamic tensions, struggles, submissions, provocations, and releases—all of which are reflected in her ceramic sculptures.

Since the 1980s, Odundo's work has defined the artist's pursuit of perfection in line and form by the continuous reworking and refining of ceramic archetypes she developed early in her career. For example, her symmetrical archetypes include bottle (fig. 14) and amphora (fig. 17) forms composed of rounded or heart-shaped bodies giving way to long, elegant necks that open outwards into dramatically flared rims. In her asymmetrical interpretations of the bottle archetype, the vessel's neck is often bowed or theatrically curved—almost swan-like (fig. 33). Odundo transforms her symmetrical amphora archetype into asymmetrical abstractions that evoke the human body, particularly the female torso. Featuring voluptuous spherical or pregnant bellies, these asymmetrical vessels markedly taper upwards and then outwards into halo-shaped openings (see fig. 9), thus emulating late nineteenth-century

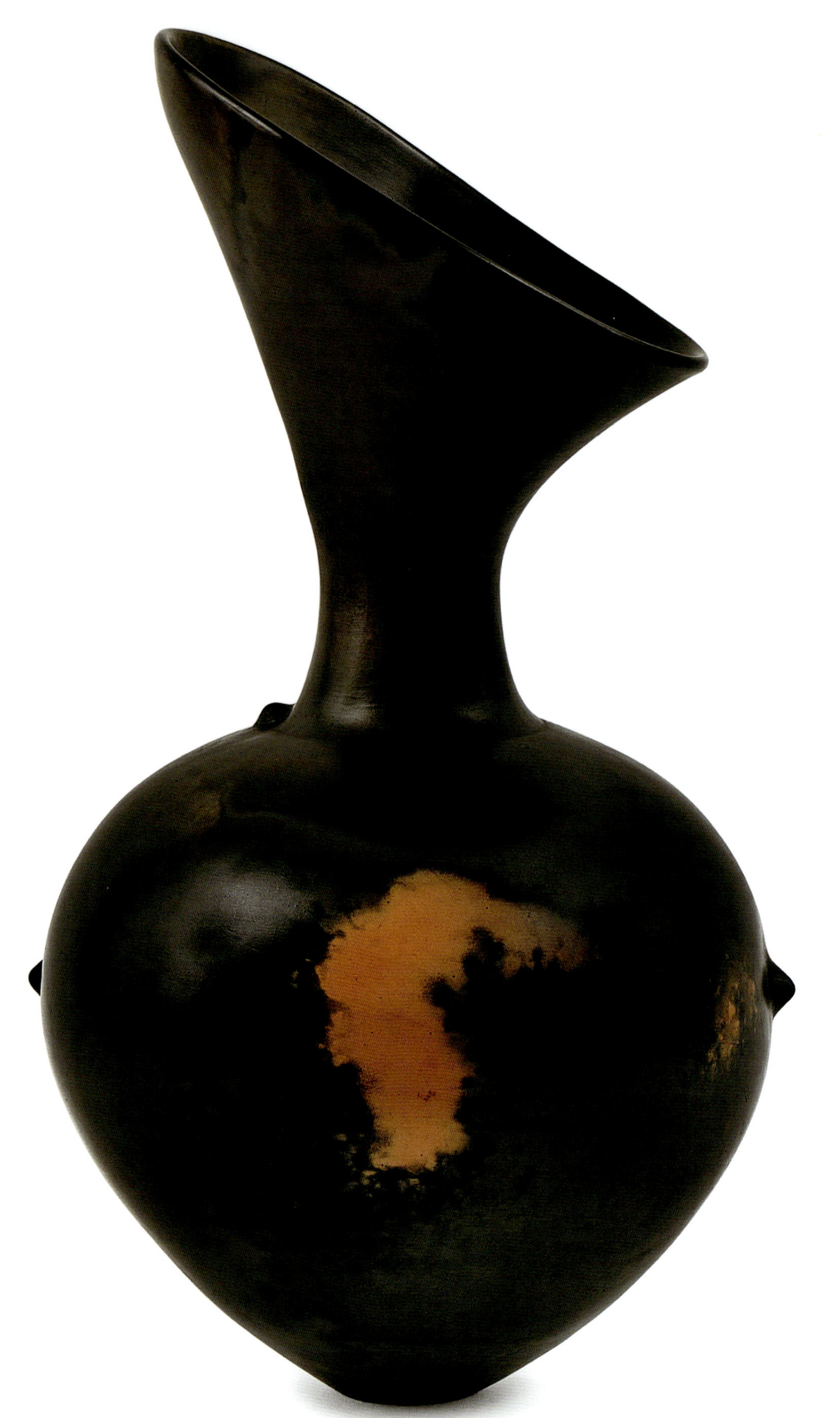

Fig. 16 Magdalene Odundo, *Untitled*,
2021. Ceramic, 51 × 30 × 29 cm

Fig. 17 Magdalene Odundo, *Untitled*,
1994. Ceramic, 47.5 × 42.8 × 42.8 cm.
National Museum of African Art,
Smithsonian Institution

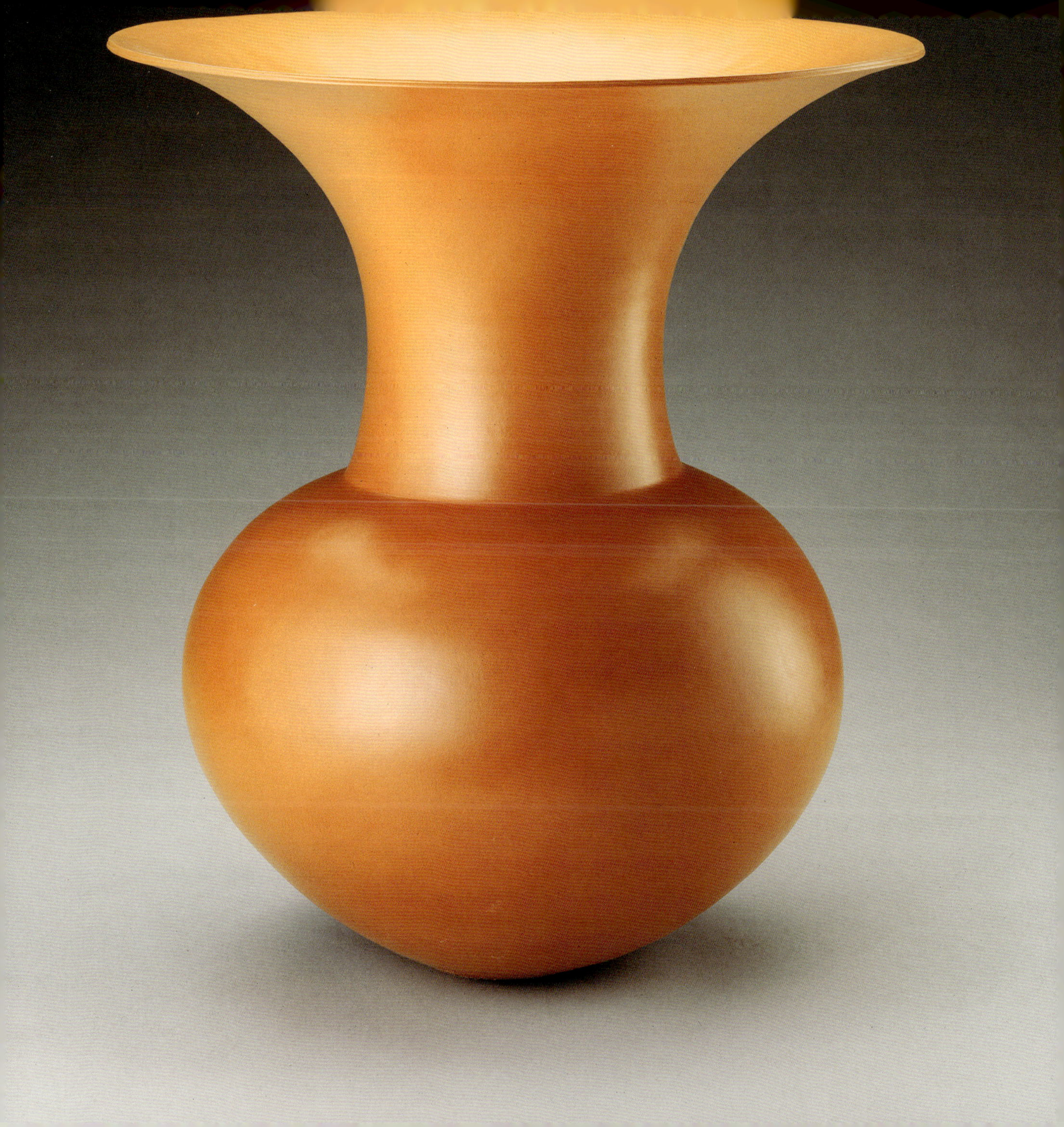

ceramics that depict the emblematic hairstyle of high-ranking Mangbetu women in southeastern Congo. While Odundo's symmetrical archetypes frequently include extravagantly proportioned loops, lugs, and protrusions, she embellishes her asymmetrical forms more reservedly, with subtle nodules strategically placed to suggest navels, breasts, or scarification markings that symbolize female beauty in many African cultures.

Exposing these hand-built vessels to multiple firings within oxygen-rich (oxidized) and oxygen-deprived (reduced) kiln atmospheres, Odundo achieves a distinctive blackened and reddish-orange lustre on her vessels. At times, serendipitous, metallic, and reddish flashings mark the surfaces, revealing the sensuous embrace of flames dancing across the slipped and smoothly burnished clay body. As Odundo explains,

> this is a process that has taken many years to learn. When the work comes out [of the kiln], it can amaze and astonish you in its beauty or it can sadden you if failing to get the right effect. I got to know my old kiln so well, however, that it eliminated the element of an alchemist's work, that chance dance with the fire. If I wanted the black ware, I would fire the vessel in a certain way and get exactly the effect I desired.[1]

After moving into her present home in Surrey in 2010, Odundo felt that this familiarity with her old kiln began to dampen her electrifying and capricious relationship with fire. Wanting to revitalize the surprising variations of hues and metallic lustre on her vessels' surfaces, she envisioned working with a different kiln, which she eventually purchased and installed at the end of 2020.[2] Despite the uncertainties and challenges of discovering its peculiarities, she quickly developed a dynamic equilibrium of power among her vision, the physics of the new kiln, the chemistry of the clay, and the heightened risk of imposing multiple firings on her pieces. As Odundo emphasizes, subjecting a single vessel to multiple firings without experience and the acquired knowledge of a kiln's impulsivity promotes a dangerous liaison that invites distortion and breakage:

> No matter how much experience you may have in controlling a kiln, in this method of multiple firings, you have to find the right equation—a balance and closeness with the alchemy of fire and the powerful and impulsive nature of the flame—to maximize its potential. This is what distinguishes the work as ceramic sculpture.

Since firing her ceramics in the new kiln, the results have been astounding, with unexpectedly bold colorations (fig. 18) compared to the subtle surface characteristics of her previous works (see fig. 29). Odundo could not have foreseen the extraordinary results that emerged from the firing or her delight in rediscovering the unpredictable dance within the firing process. "It has liberated me!" she rejoices, admitting that firing is her least favourite

Fig. 18 Magdalene Odundo, *Untitled*, 2019. Ceramic, 56.5 × 36 × 33 cm

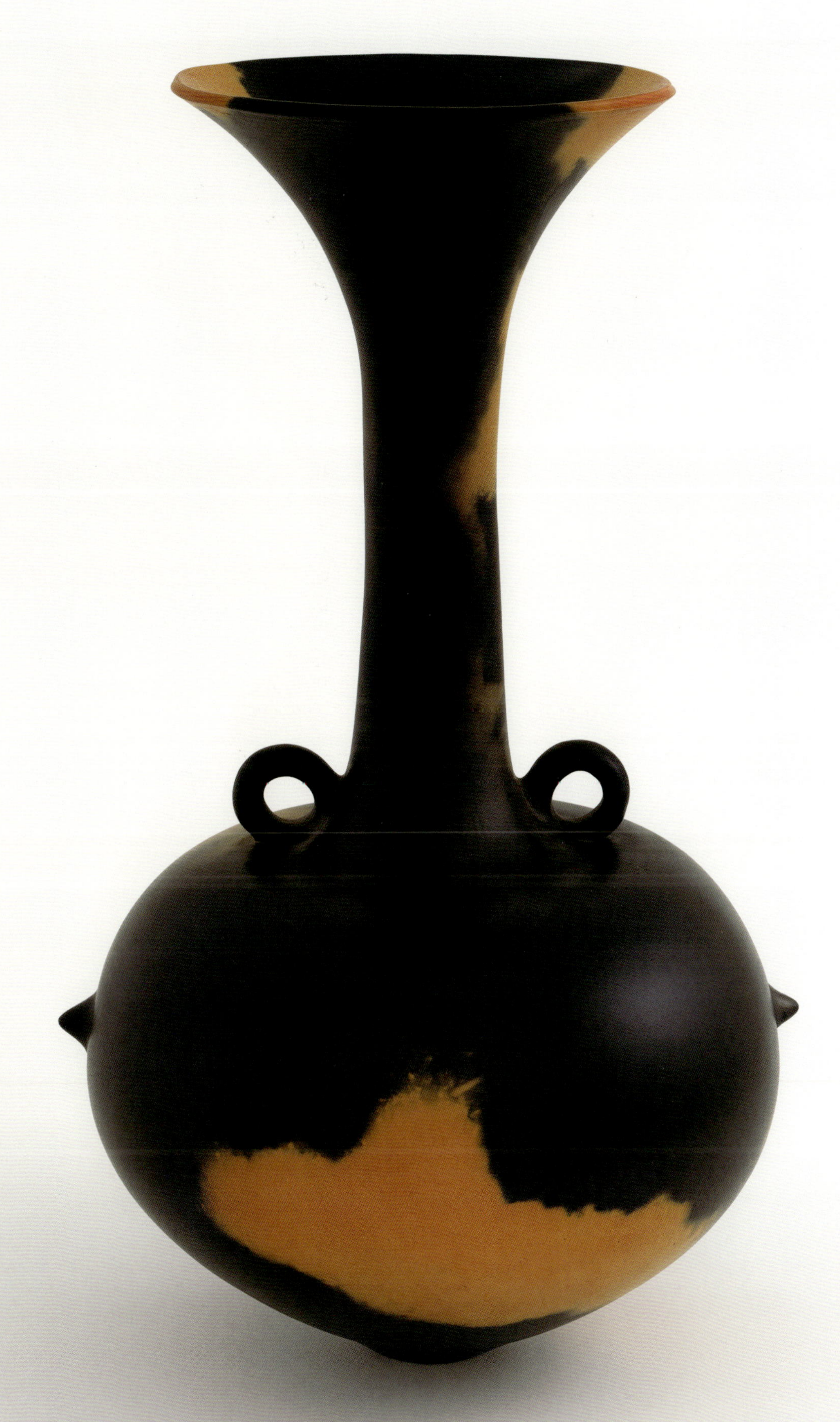

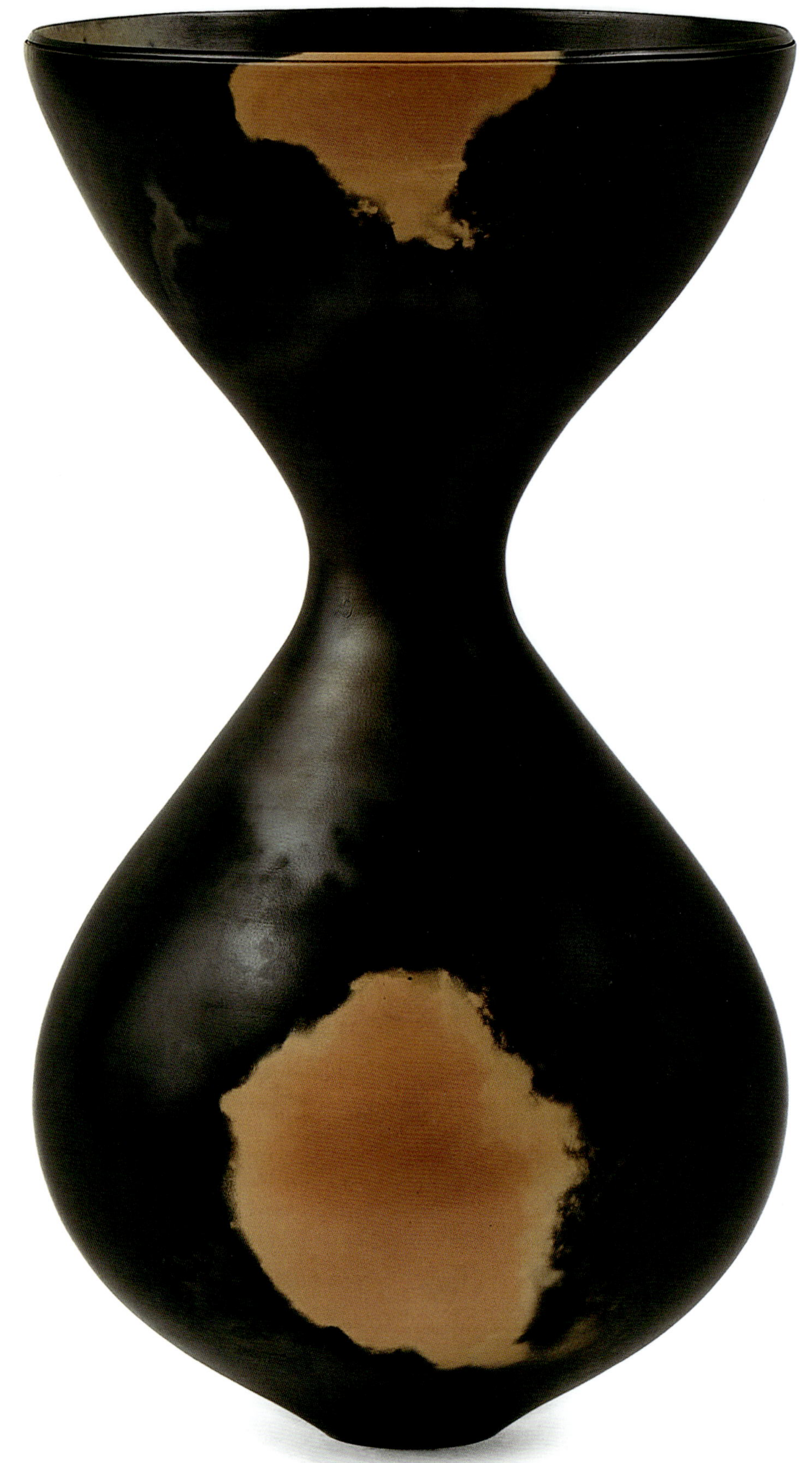

aspect in the process of making ceramics, though "it is a necessary evil." While hand building a vessel, Odundo cultivates a very
tactile relationship with the plasticity of the clay. During the firing
process, the physical detachment from the clay offers her an
uncomfortable disconnect in that relationship, one that contra-
dicts the tangible experience of the hands-on forming of clay
into a vessel.

Odundo's recent works reveal the budding relationship
between the artist and the dynamics of working with an unfamiliar
kiln, with all the intimacies, surprises, crises, and resolutions that
accompany such nascent liaisons. The vessel surfaces unexpectedly depart from the characteristically subtle gradations of colour
and flashings in her earlier work. Their bold, stark contrast of
oxidized and reduced colours exhibit a startling vitality, with
lustrous, deep black grounds and clearly defined fields of reddish-
orange flashings that evoke the glow of continents, islands, and
peninsulas surrounded by the dark ocean on a moonless night
(fig. 19). These vessels display a surprising symmetry between
the artist's vision and her control of the kiln's temperament,
not only indicating Odundo's vast experience, familiarity with
the properties of the clay, and maturity as a ceramic artist but
also noticeably revealing how her use of a larger kiln has empow-
ered and encouraged her to create much taller pieces, some
commanding a magnificent stature ranging between 50 and
60 centimetres.

Since expanding her home-based studio in the idyllic Surrey
countryside, completing construction in March 2020, Odundo
relishes the present "glorious space," with its amazing height and
light-filled, expansive windows that look out to the quiet garden
behind her home. "Gone are the restrictions I had in a smaller
workshop," she notes. In this larger, meditational space, the artist
can engage with and move around the pieces with greater agility,
pushing the limits of the clay and the sizes of the pieces, and
embracing the increased risks for mistakes and disappointments
to occur while firing. "I can now walk tall—and proud—while
working on my tiptoes," the artist laughs, acknowledging that
these significant changes in the studio milieu have bestowed her
with greater confidence and forthrightness in the advancement of
her ceramic art.

Odundo's newfound boldness is especially evident in her
recent vessels, through which she unequivocally challenges the
physics of size, proportion, and balance—as is her signature
style—while continuing to heed her self-imposed stringency of
upholding the purity of line and form. As with the archetypes she
first developed in the late 1980s and early 1990s, her newer
vessels also feature evocative nodules (fig. 16) and strategically
positioned lugs or ringed "handles" (see fig. 36) but are now more
diminutively proportioned. Like her earlier oeuvre, the vessels are
perfectly poised on a dainty base, which then voluptuously
expands outwards and contracts into a heart-shaped, sensuous
body but with now even more dramatically cinched waistlines

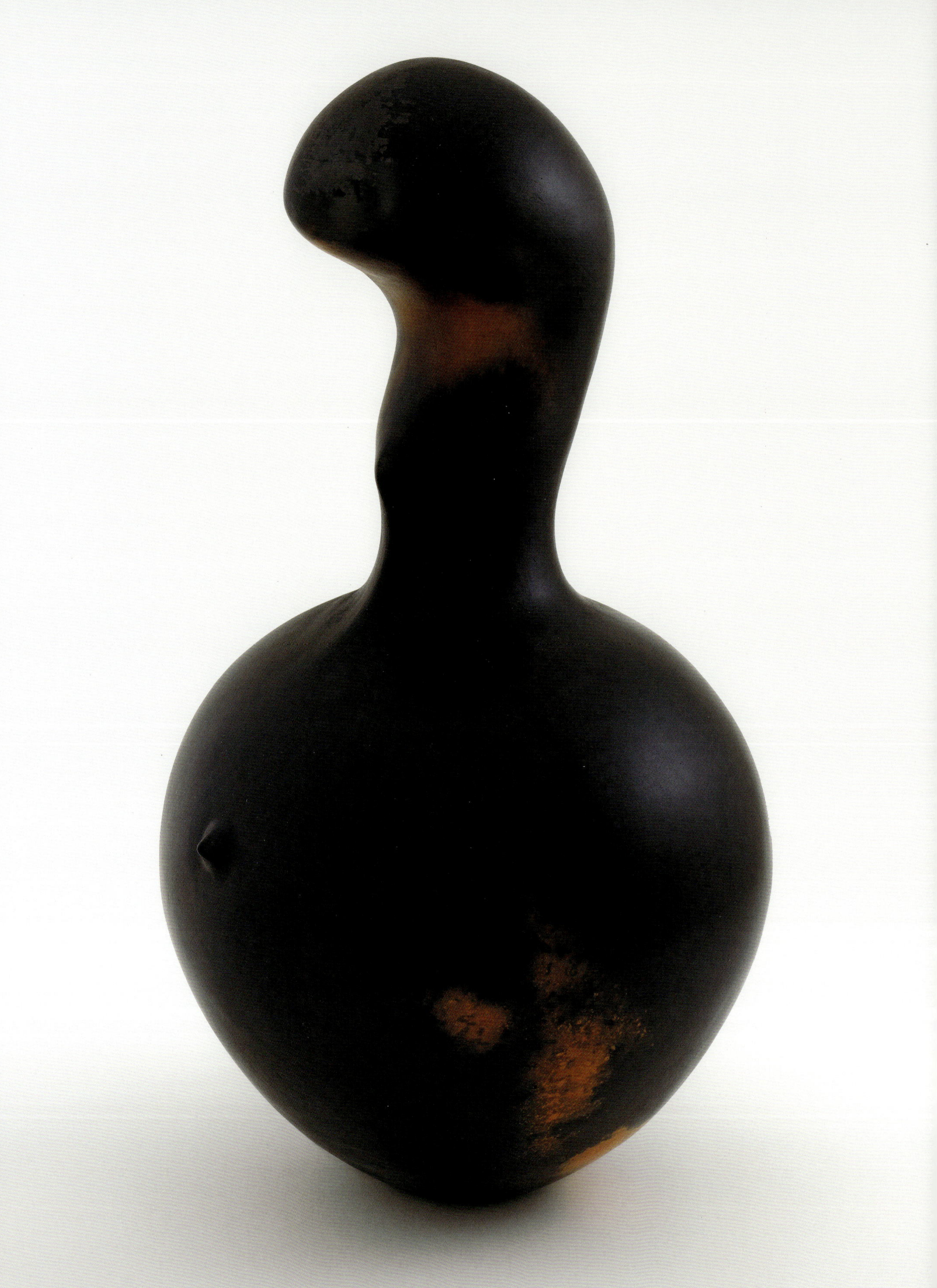

(fig. 25), reminiscent of the fashions of the Victorian bustle era of the 1870s and 1880s.

These vessels exude an exhilaration and audaciousness that belies the artist's personal battle in recent years with a serious illness that began in 2017 and led to loss of sensation in her fingertips, which in hand-built ceramics is critical in manipulating and moving with the plasticity of the clay. Following a forced two-year hiatus from her ceramic art, Odundo captured the essence of her struggles with—and ultimately her victory over—serious physical ailment in the form of an asymmetrical vessel (fig. 20). This extraordinary sculpture exhibits a conspicuously organic and contorted silhouette. "It's a very unusual piece, really," Odundo affirms, further noting that it was the first piece she made in 2020 and marked a new direction in her work:

> After regrouping physically, mentally, and intellectually from my illness, I wondered how I was going to come back to my work, especially after the success of my retrospective exhibition [*Magdalene Odundo: The Journey of Things*] at the Hepworth Wakefield in 2019. I became introspective, critically examining pieces I had completed before my illness, and learning to accept and adapt to my new body. These contorted pieces came through from a place of relearning how to "be" with my work and how to reuse my hands and body differently.

Through this piece, Odundo addressed her need to heal, or perhaps was searching to be healed through the vessel. "It was as if I was giving myself a mission to get better. But I was struggling with it. The vessel was contorting because *I* was contorting." Odundo had intended to create a more organic reinterpretation of her Mangbetu archetype vessel from 2001.[3] As she describes,

> I was trying to negotiate with, speak with, and dance with [this earlier version]. But it just was not going right; I was going all over the place with it. So I felt I needed to go back and reconnect with it, to contain that power within the vessel. It was as if I was commissioning someone to make me a healing pot, a medicine pot to give to the *mganga*, a pot that contains the power to heal just like medicinal therapies.

Odundo's reference to the *mganga* (Swahili for traditional healer) recalls the ancestral ways of many Central, Southern, and East African Bantu cultures, including her own in Kenya, where people suffering from misfortune and illness commission spiritual healers to create medicine pots. Made from clay, gourds, animal horns, shells, or other readily available receptacles, these symbolically charged containers give tangible form to spirit powers. Healers, or *waganga*, then use such spirit containers to aid in a person's recovery from misfortunes caused by destabilized power structures, especially (but not exclusively) between the physical and spiritual worlds.

Odundo directly engages with this concept of the "spirit pot" and the potency of the vessel as a powerful healing mechanism.

Fig. 20 Magdalene Odundo, *Untitled*, 2020. Ceramic, 59 × 35 × 31 cm

With this goal in mind, she departed from her characteristically open vessel form by closing the crown, leaving only a subtle opening at the back of the head, which bends dramatically forward, as if weighted by taxing thoughts, sadness, or mournful emotions. Through this healing vessel, Odundo—like the *mganga*—captured, contained, and controlled the debilitating energy that was hindering her recovery, blocking the pathway back to her dance with clay and fire. "Closing the vessel just released me," she exalted.

> It released all the tensions pent up inside after months of lying flat and helpless in a hospital bed. In fact, a lot of this new work came from learning and evaluating whether I could still work with clay using the same diligence and degree of graphic discipline that I apply to each piece… and wondering if I could regain feeling in my fingertips enough to reconnect with my method of working with the geography of clay. I have had to work much harder now to maintain that same strictness that I impose on my work.

While working on this asymmetrical vessel, Odundo encountered a new sensibility in her fingers and body, galvanizing her cadenced dance with the medium of clay and opening up a pathway that led to the two symmetrical vessels with "their hands on their hips" (fig. 18, fig. 36). "There was a great joy in trying to control these symmetrical forms. I wanted them to reflect the notion of arising from and triumphing over struggle," she exclaims. These perfectly poised vessels feature long necks that extend demonstratively upwards and outwards before unfolding into Odundo's characteristically wide, flaring rims, personifying triumph through their exuberant and uplifting acrobatic dance, and echoing the artist's new freedom in working with clay again. As Odundo explains,

> I was looking back to that symmetrical archetype, with the raised neck and hands on the hips, which revisits an image of a pair of gossiping ladies, such as washerwomen gathering or hanging laundry, who stand back, strike a stance of repose with hands on their hips, and admire their finished work. They are like dancers who are *en pointe* and then descend onto their heels after the twirling and pirouetting is done. Motionless, they catch their breath and take pride in a job well done.

Odundo's drawings of humanized vessels leaning in toward each other—as if sharing a secret—clearly evoke this metaphorical image (see fig. 51).

Like the artist's personal growth in the last several years, her most recent series of "gossiping ladies" have grown taller, prouder, and bolder. "There is no more mournfulness about them," she declared. Indeed, the elation embodied by these newer works resonates with the artist's rediscovery of hope and the unflinching sense of relief, gratitude, and joy in her outspoken existential decree: "Oh, thank God I'm alive!"

Fig. 21 Magdalene Odundo, *Untitled*, 2016–2017. Ceramic, 53.7 × 29.8 × 29.8 cm

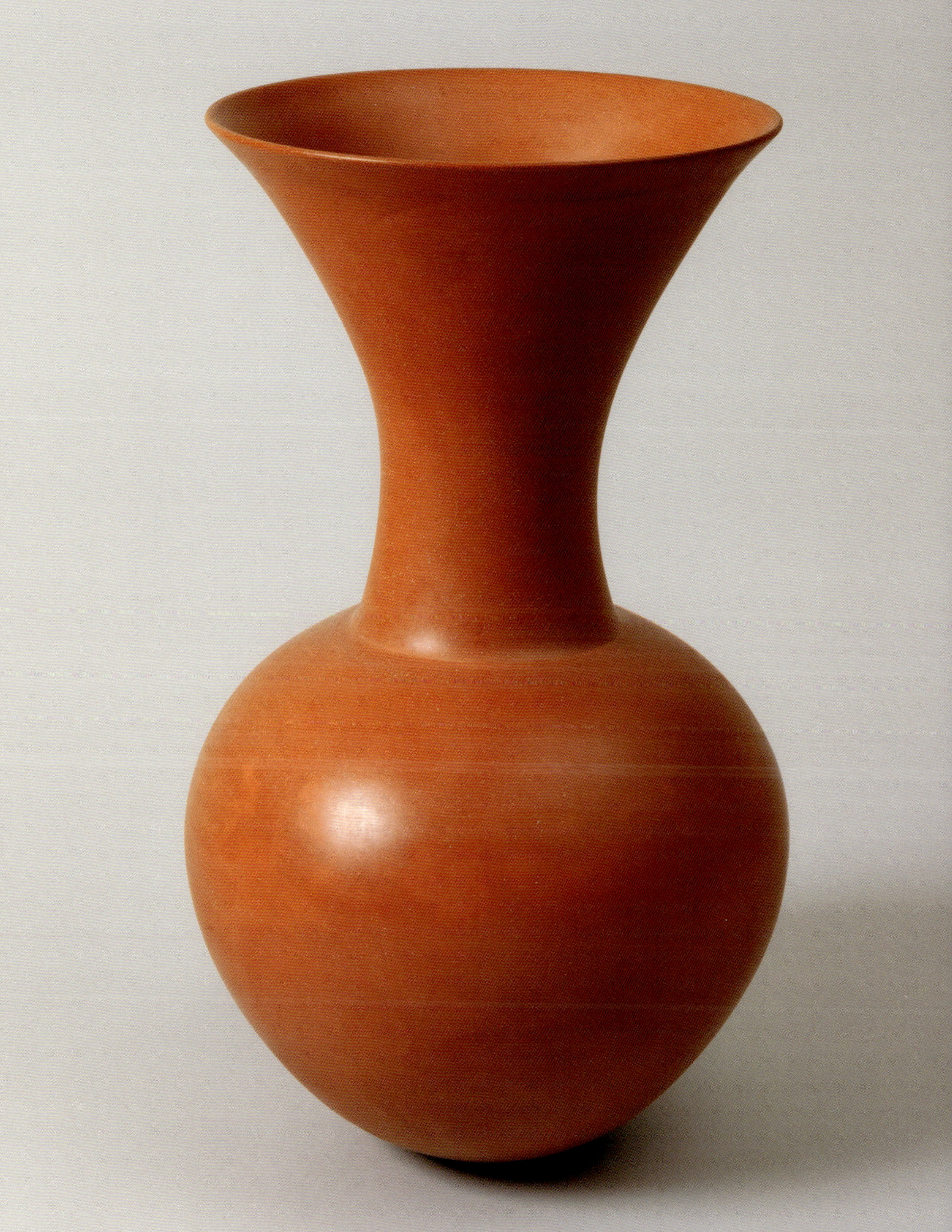

When considering the vessels she has made since her recovery from illness, one must account for their context. This was a time marked by unprecedented social isolation and the colossal loss of human life due to the global COVID-19 pandemic. It was a time characterized by a dangerously unstable world filled with heightened awareness of systemic racial injustice, social and economic inequities, and escalating geopolitical posturing. One cannot help but wonder whether Odundo's jubilant symmetrical vessels manifest her search for balance in an increasingly unhinged world. "It has been an odd year," she agrees, "and we are living in a massively contorted world. But at the same time, these challenging times help us appreciate the little things we have, and you can see this play itself out in my new vessels."

Odundo's reflections upon the Black Lives Matter movement, for example, are indicative of her sense of déjà vu and, by extension, her exasperation about the continued racial discrimination plaguing the world today:

> I grew up in a colonial Kenya, where racial injustices took place all the time. The colonial government selected Black security forces specifically from particular ethnic groups to round up, humiliate, and beat other "natives" and to remove the men from the villages into detention camps. This policy deliberately intended to pit one ethnic group against another, thus dividing the people and strengthening the colonial agenda. The racial injustice we have all witnessed in the United States—and elsewhere—is a continuation of the same "divide and conquer" tactics. The repetition of racial discrimination, the subjugation of particular groups of peoples, and the clemency towards others are embedded in the neo-colonial mind-set.
>
> Living outside the confinements of colonialism, I find ways in which I *can* negotiate these constraints [of racism] within the framework of making art that speaks to a particular time. As an artist, there is no other language than the visual language to explain yourself to those who have lost "the empire" or who justify maintaining their superiority over others by subjugating them. So, in my work, I try to embody the notion of being proud of who you are and refusing to be discriminated against or of negotiating ourselves within the framework of that discrimination. I have this dogged stubbornness and refuse *not* to have my work recognized for what it is. However, being aware that I am here because of what is happening on my behalf and because of what I have done through my contributions—however small—to this liberation is why I delight in working today…of being in the here and now, at this moment, and in this place, being able to assert myself through ceramic vessels that can speak a universal language of purity, simplicity, and balance.

In this context, Odundo's use of clay as "a universal language" underscores her desire—and "greatest challenge," she adds—for her art to contain a wholeness yet also a simplicity that allows each vessel to have an emotive autonomy and express what words cannot, in a visual language that speaks to all, regardless of their origins. Her more recent vessels are confident, outspoken, and fluent in their emotive language, and like Odundo today, they are wiser, stronger, and bolder than their quiet, contemplative predecessors, unveiling the kind of dignity of being in the here and now that commands space, voice, and expression. Yet with the retrospective knowledge and the wisdom that comes only with the passage of time, these radiant, more mature sculpted "ladies" also invite deliberation on what it means to be present and mindful, to rediscover well-being and triumph, to negotiate and overcome the adversities of our time, and, especially, to strive for balance in our current world with "all its oddities, contortions, and injustices."

Notes

1. All quotes in this essay are from an interview that the author conducted with Magdalene Odundo, April 25, 2021.

2. This kiln is a German Rohde KG 750A Gas Frontloader, 750 litres, for temperatures up to 1320°C.

3. This particular vessel, now in the collection of the Hood Museum of Art at Dartmouth College (C.2003.50), is related to a work from 2005–2006 (fig. 15).

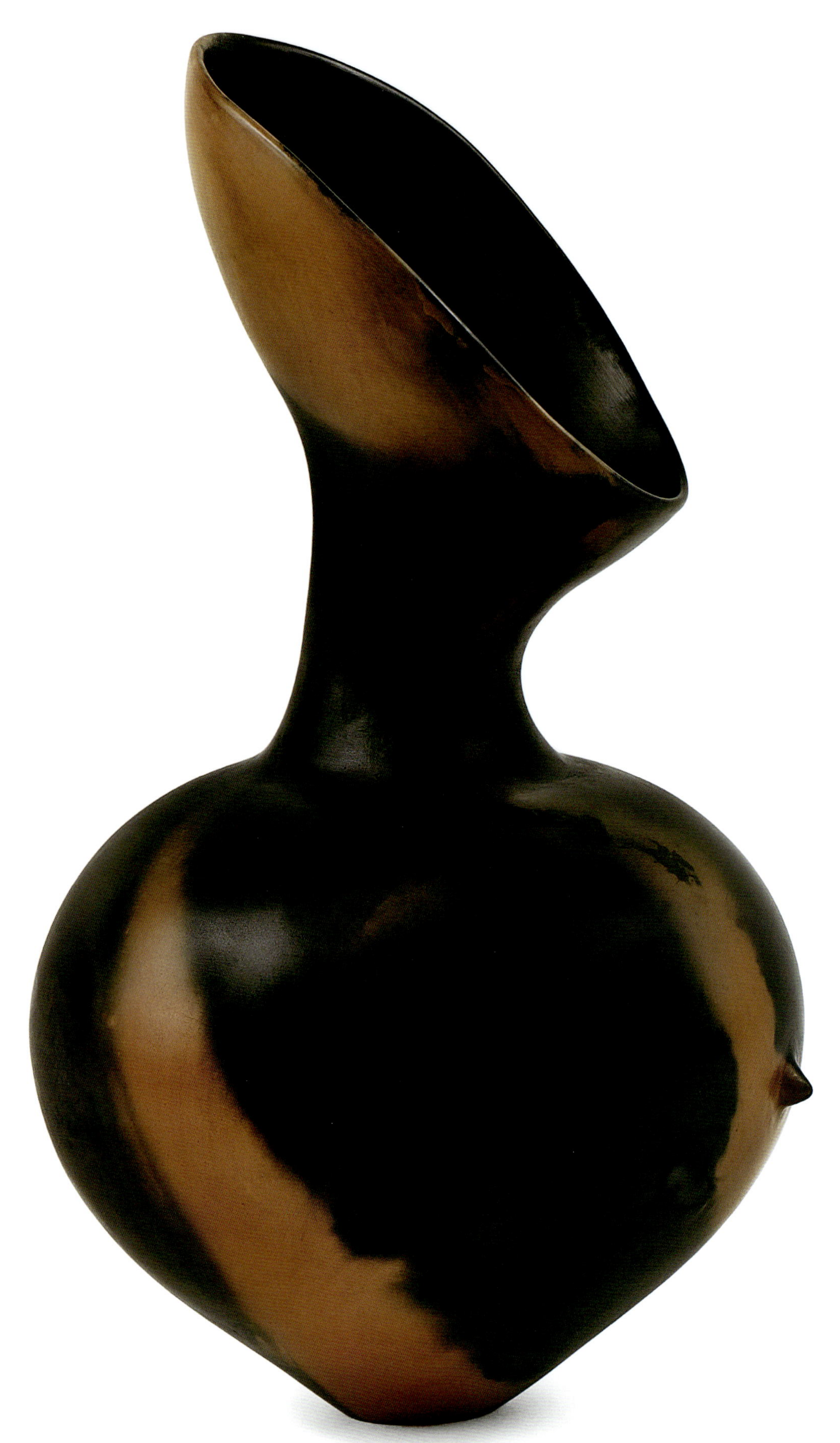

 Magdalene Odundo, *Untitled*,
2021. Ceramic, 53 × 33 × 33.5 cm

Fig. 23 Magdalene Odundo, *Untitled*,
2022. Ceramic, 58 × 24 × 24 cm

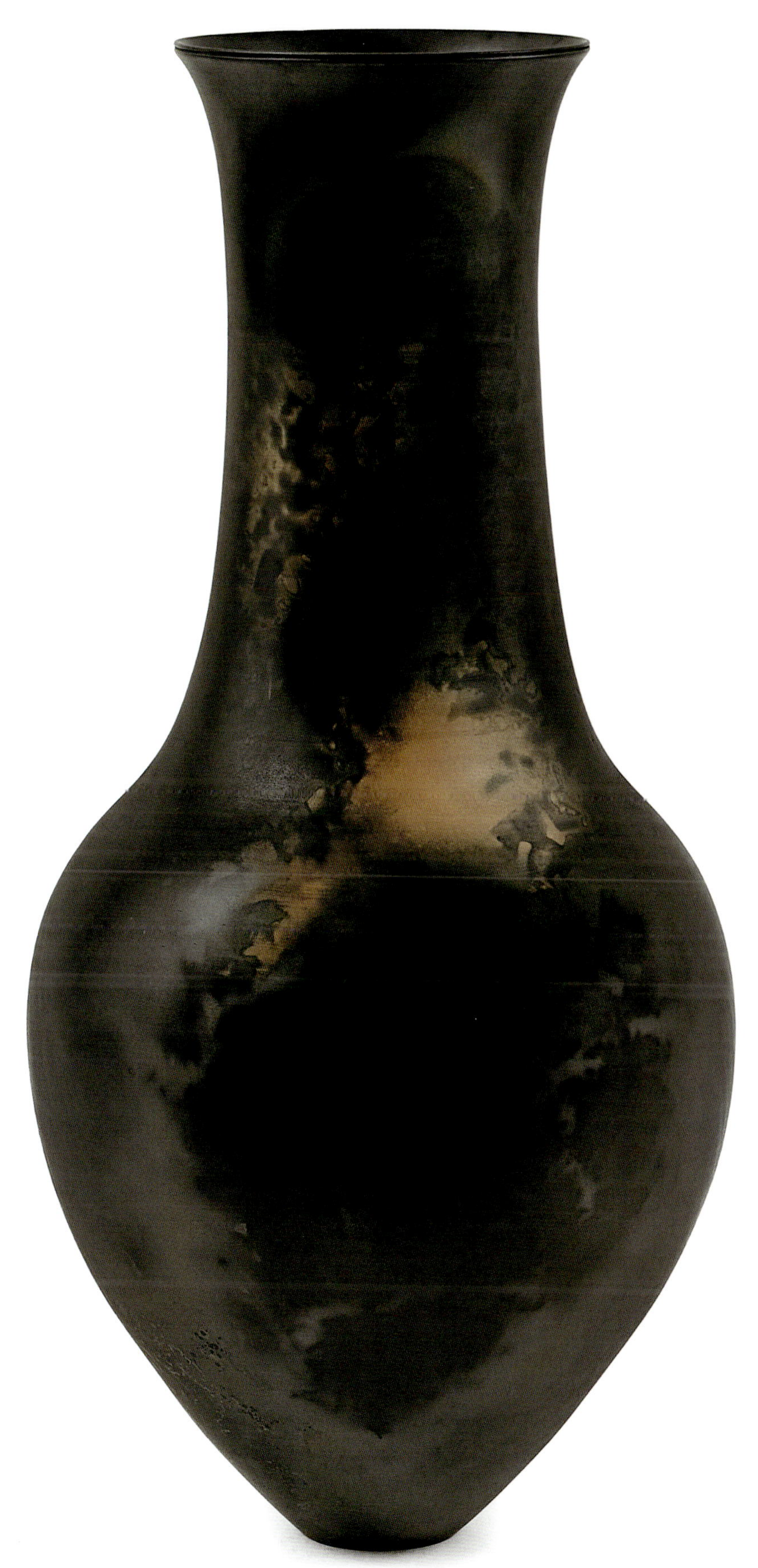

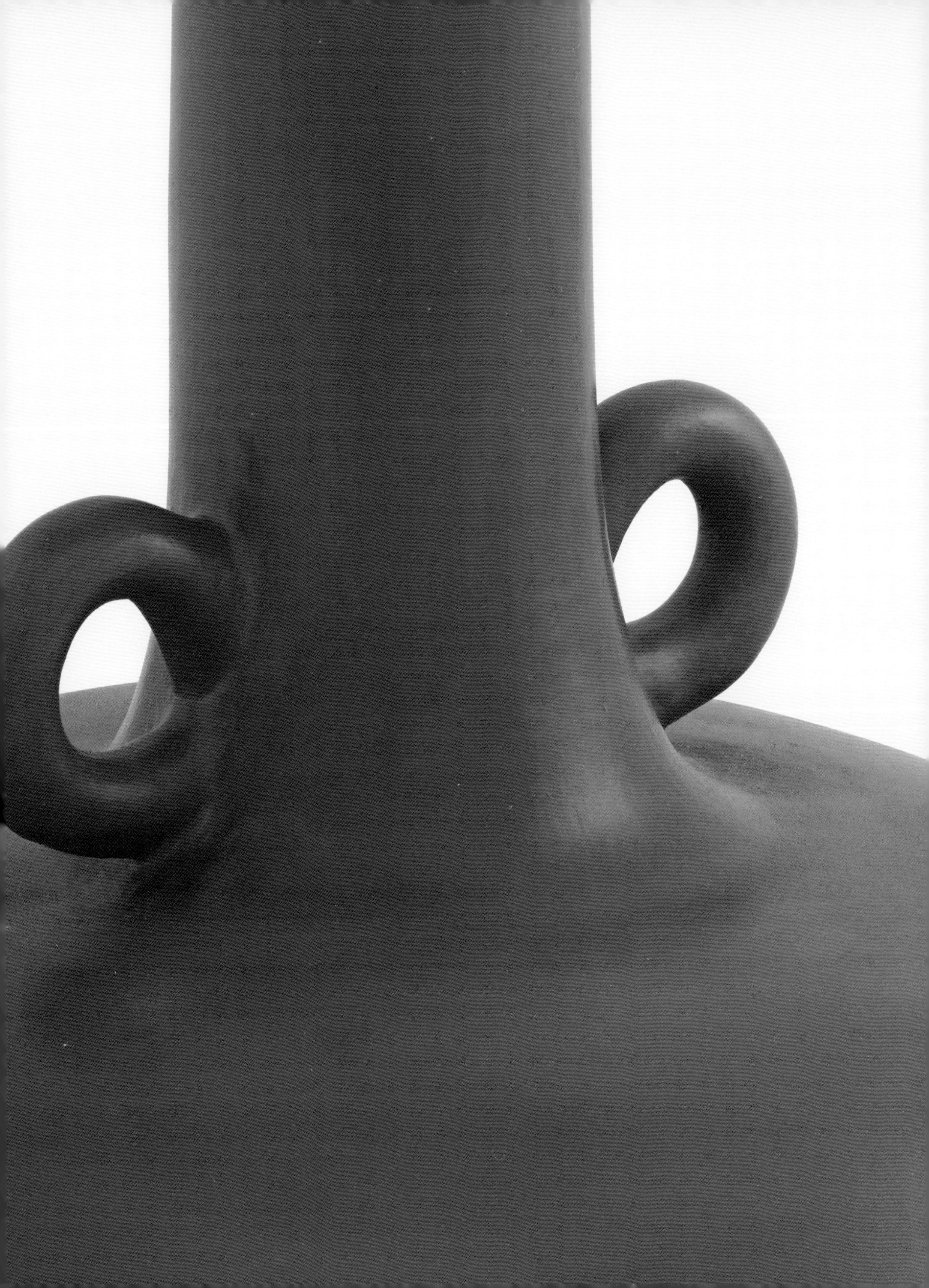

Elizabeth Harney

Transhistorical Conversations
Magdalene Odundo and Global Contemporary Art

Many critics and curators have been attracted to the oscillating spatial-temporal logics of Odundo's clay vessels, which draw from a mix of African, Indigenous, Japanese, Greco-Roman, and European sources and seem to embody a multiplicity of worlds. Their restrained economy of form, burnished patinas, and intimate scale activate a visual culture memory bank we didn't know we had (fig. 16). Indeed, there is an uncanny familiarity to these sleek, sensuous pieces, which resemble not simply everyday vessels but also living bodies and spirits. Odundo has teased that they are "able to hear each other, speak to each other and create friction while intimating—don't touch."[1] And yet, except in her figurative silk screens (fig. 45) and sketches, these bodies, suggested by volume and minimalist form alone, remain tantalizingly absent.

The cosmopolitan, polyvalent, and multitemporal character of these enigmatic works seems tailor-made for our current "global contemporary" art moment. The quietude of Odundo's pieces offers a salve for our intensely chaotic contemporary era. And yet their fragility, arrested dynamism, and deeply worked patina rely upon the unpredictability and ambiguity of the firing process. As curator Augustus Casely-Hayford puts it, Odundo's work "is like a compass, offering . . . a way of navigating geography and history and a range of very complex issues that feel very much [a] part of what is happening today."[2]

Odundo is understandably drawn to historical and modern objects that suggest certain anthropomorphic qualities. Those that

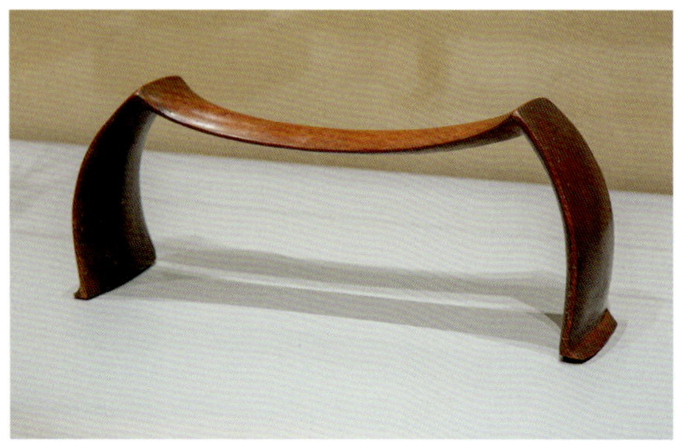

elicit a sense of movement and presence, with temporality arrested, such as a perfectly designed Tongan headrest that uses only the forms necessary to preserve an elaborate coiffure and accommodate the motion required to achieve quiet rest, captivate her attention (fig. 24).

Her pieces live within and move through multiple cultural economies: British crafts, ceramics, spiritual and commemorative objects, fine arts, and African and diasporic arts. These categorical slippages, similar to those employed by other contemporary artists such as El Anatsui and Yinka Shonibare, demand multiple interpretative frames within the museum, the market, and the academy.

Of the same generation as British diasporic artists like Sonia Boyce, Lubaina Himid, and Veronica Ryan, Odundo resisted easy co-option into the Black arts movement of the 1980s and 1990s, which galvanized around political debates addressing difference and (in)visibility in the British art world.[3] With a childhood spent between Kenya and India, Odundo arrived in England decades after those whom Stuart Hall has called "the last colonials," who immigrated in the 1940s and 1950s.[4] Odundo's travels for familial and educational reasons are well-documented now, as are her frequent and sustained visits to the storerooms and display cases of museums to think through form and material from a wide array of global sources.[5] But less attention has been paid to the parallels between her intellectual and creative trajectory and that of many members of this earlier generation of artists, activists, and intellectuals from the African continent. Artists such as Ben Enwonwu, Bertina Lopes, Ernest Mancoba, Iba N'Diaye, and Gerard Sekoto were dedicated modernists and anti-colonialists having affiliations and associations with multiple communities and histories of practice; but above all, much like Odundo, they were universalists. As Hall explains,

> They came…feeling that they naturally belonged to the modern movement and, in a way, it belonged to them. The promise of decolonization fired their ambition, their sense of themselves as already "modern persons." It liberated them from any lingering sense of inferiority. Their aim was to engage the modern world as equals on its own terrain.[6]

Their own writings attest to the important role their frequent visits to ethnographic/colonial collections and fine art museums played in understanding their craft.[7] In this regard, they were no different from any artist set on consuming as much visual and material knowledge as possible. However, these visits were instrumental in providing at times their only access to a pan-African heritage that colonial authorities had sought to destroy or delegitimize.

I situate Odundo's story in relation to these earlier modernist histories in part to anticipate the retrospective work inherent to our

Fig. 24 Unidentified Tonga maker, Headrest, Tonga, early 20th century. Wood, 41.6 × 11.8 × 17 cm. Royal Ontario Museum

Fig. 25 Magdalene Odundo, *Untitled*, 2022. Ceramic, 42 × 22 × 22 cm

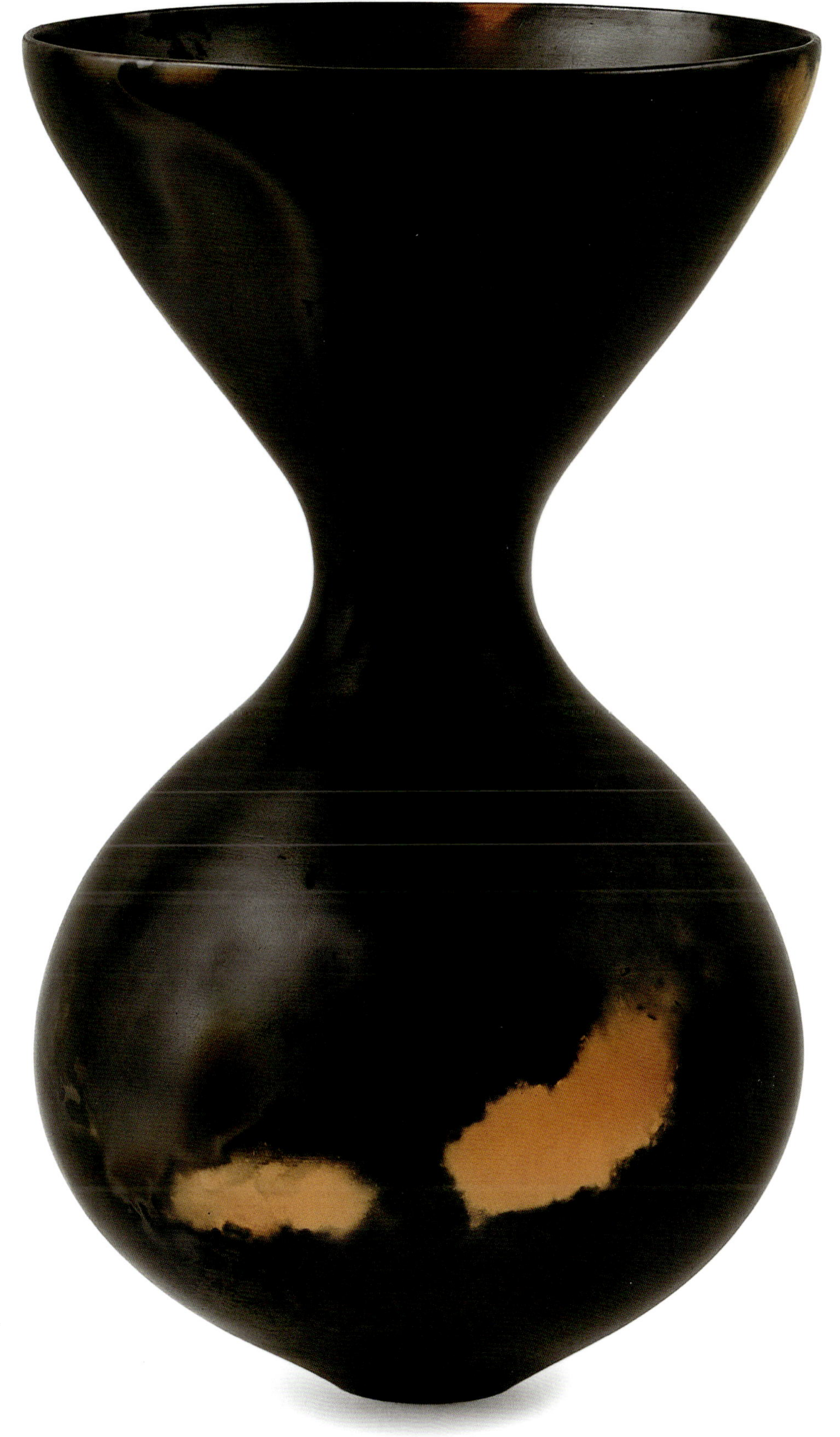

era of global contemporary art practice, curation, and criticism.[8] To consider Odundo's supposedly timeless forms within a global contemporary framework is a fraught affair, for its very posthistorical premise threatens to misread her deeply archaeological practice and her visceral attachment to material that is also, in the end, a commitment to shared humanity. The art world today is also often too quick to assume our contemporary moment has produced worldly relations that have no precedent, but the movements of African and diasporic modernists suggest otherwise. For Odundo, "historical and contemporary work can be viewed as a continuum…as in fine art throughout the world, classical and historical can, and does, inform the contemporary, while the contemporary reinterprets, and moves on."[9]

With the seismic political, economic, and cultural shifts following the end of the Cold War and the reordering of international power after 9/11, art theorists and curators began to stress a shared state of "contemporaneity," a condition that supposedly relieved the art world from the burdens of history.[10] Powered by an ever-expanding list of international biennales, blockbuster exhibitions, and art fairs, curators, scholars, and critics struggled to make sense of this post–Cold War, late capitalist world—one seemingly unfettered by history and organized by a rapacious neoliberal system. With one world system, they argued, artists whose work had previously been siloed in ethnographic, vernacular, or postcolonial spaces, in both the market and the museum world, could operate on the level playing field of "the contemporary."[11]

In the first decades of the twenty-first century, this new vision—resolutely global and posthistorical—led to numerous high-profile, multimillion-dollar productions, such as the Tate Triennial of 2009 and the 2011 exhibition *The Global Contemporary: Art Worlds after 1989*, which claimed to sketch out a "new world map of art," unencumbered by modernist history, noting that:

> In many developing countries, art can only be contemporary because locally *it has no modern history*. Thus, the twenty-first century is seeing the worldwide emergence of an art that lays claim to contemporaneity without limits and without history.[12]

But is the global contemporary a style, an approach, a school, or an -ism? Writing in 2009, Hal Foster disabused us of our search for clarity here, arguing that "in its very heterogeneity, much present practice seems to float free of historical determination, conceptual definition, and critical judgment."[13]

The discursive space of "contemporary African art," emerging within the broader terrain of the "global contemporary" and advanced by important African and diasporic curatorial and critical voices, including Salah Hassan, Koyo Kouoh, Simon Njami, and the late Okwui Enwezor and Bisi Silva, to name but a few, does coalesce around conceptual (often lens-based) and installation works. It has also opened a much-needed revision of histories of modernity (and modernism), with calls for restitution and repair for colonial-era mistreatment of peoples, objects, and cultures. The paradox at the heart of this new cultural condition is that it is at once posthistorical and characterized by deeply archival or archaeological artistic practices that reckon with modernity's violence and issue urgent calls for decolonization along with a reinvestment in shared futures.

In Eddy Firmin's work, chosen by Odundo for this exhibition, ⌂ *(Research/Hunting)* (2016; fig. 26), the Guadeloupean-Canadian artist, utilizes the trope of the mask, a fetish of authenticity in the traditional African art market, both as a vessel for cultural memories that had been strangled by the yoke of colonialism and as a reminder that the power wielded by a global fashion conglomerate like Chanel is intimately linked to earlier, modernist forms of racial capitalism and, indeed, contemporary forms of inequality. Melding traditional with contemporary, in form, design, and material, Firmin's practice has obvious affinities to that of Odundo and, like hers, his work complicates any easy "global contemporary framework."

What does all the discursive wrangling mean for understanding the impact and import of Odundo's worldly practice today, or indeed this exhibition at the Gardiner for which she is both co-curator and artist? Perhaps we should be heeding John Picton's words, who mused many years ago, "In the end, of course, the question really should not be how do we (ethnographers, curators, art historians) place Magdalene Odundo, how do we fit her in; but, rather, is this a matter of any concern to her?"[14]

As a diasporic artist in England, Odundo is haunted by the ghosts of the triangle trade, racial capitalism, and empire. The spoils of that violence have filled the storerooms in which she has worked; the arrogance of empire has carved out networks of trade that forcibly moved not only bodies but also humble, everyday objects and ideas of making. As an artist, a researcher, and an educator, Odundo has always adopted the multitemporal approach cited by contemporary theorists, pushing us to acknowledge the fruits of interrelated material histories and the universality of clay. For her 2019 exhibition *The Journey of Things*, at the Hepworth Wakefield in Yorkshire, she defied linear history by including alongside her own works diverse historical and contemporary objects and artworks.[15]

It is of little surprise then that for the current exhibition the artist chose to include work by the late Trinidadian Canadian abstract painter Denyse Thomasos (fig. 12). Thomasos addressed the transhistorical trauma of enslavement and contemporary experiences of exile and racism through an intense use of line, scale, and colour that dealt "with bodies and how they're confined in the spaces they inhabit."[16] In similar fashion, Odundo's works suggest the presence of bodies—their curves, gestures, and labours (fig. 29). These labours involve everyday living, the making of pots, the honouring of

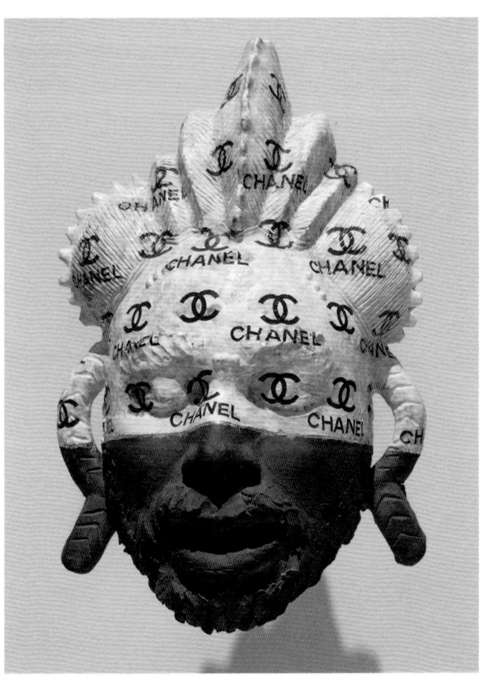

Fig. 26 Eddy Firmin, ⌂ *(Research/ Hunting)*, 2016. Ceramic, 16 × 13 × 8 cm. Gardiner Museum

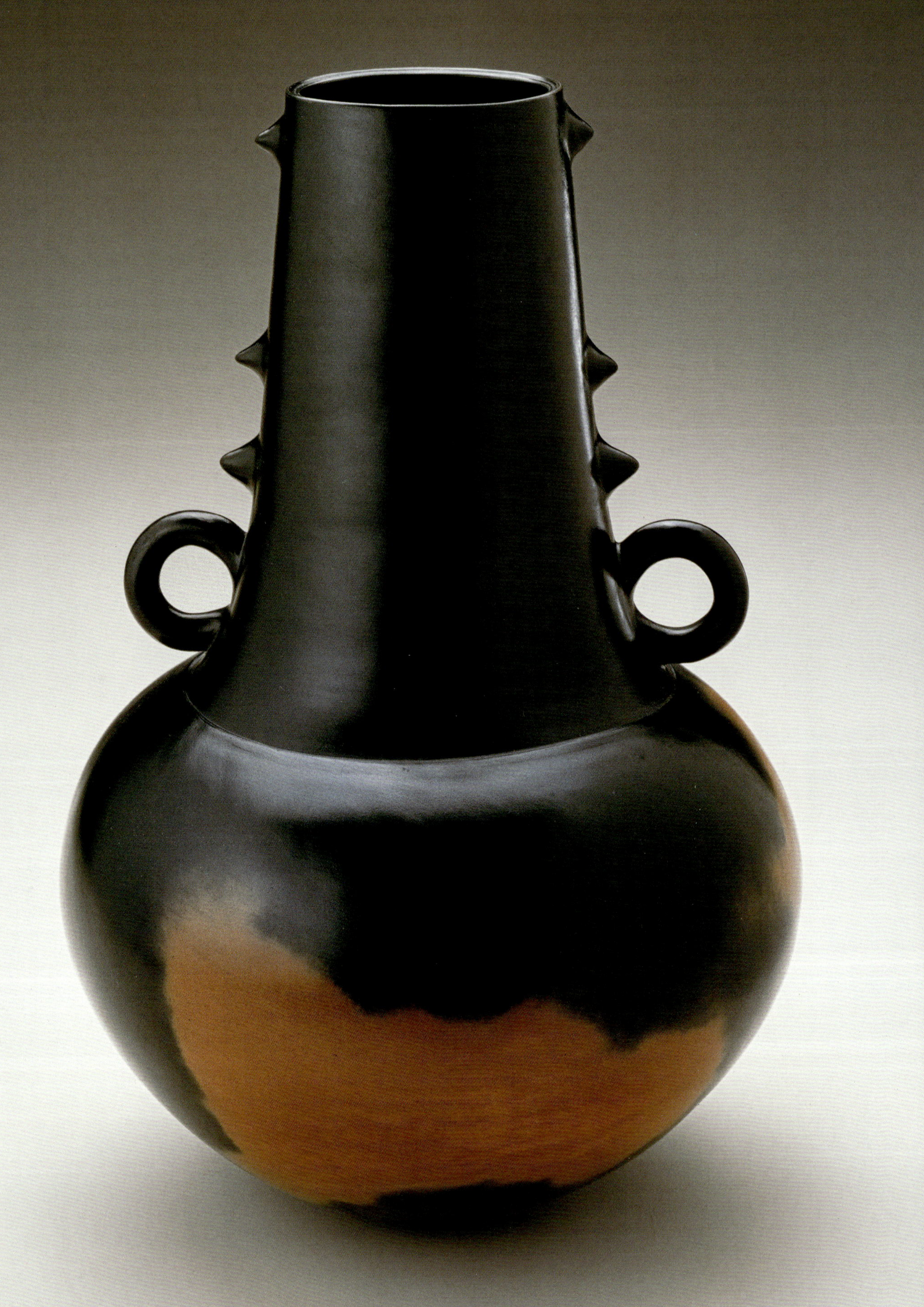

Fig. 27 Magdalene Odundo, *Untitled,*
1990. Ceramic, 35.2 × 24 × 24 cm.
National Museum of African Art,
Smithsonian Institution

Fig. 28a (left) Oluseye, *Ploughing
Liberty #18*, 2021. Found farm tool, hockey
stick, brass dowel, 178 × 23 × 24 cm.
Dr. Kenneth Montague | The Wedge
Collection

Fig. 28b (right) Oluseye, *Ploughing
Liberty #16*, 2021. Found farm tool, hockey
stick, brass dowel, 178 × 20 × 20 cm.
Collection of John Donald

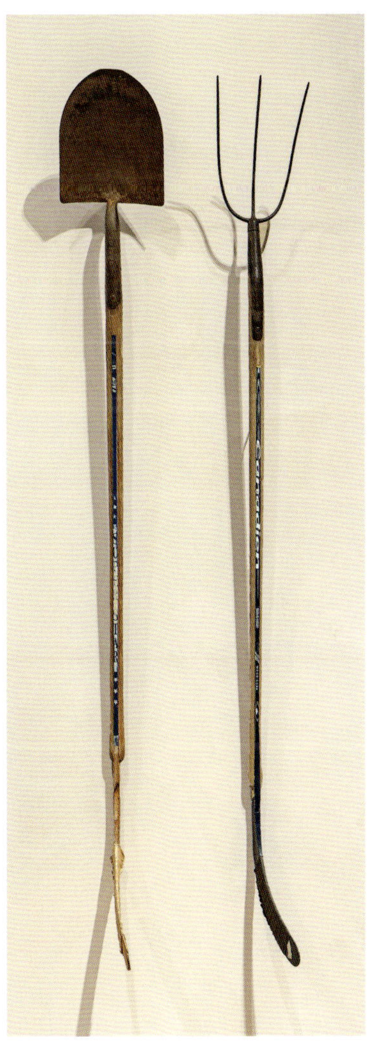

ancestors, and the nurturing of family, but her vessels also point us quietly towards an inescapable politics and history of forced labour and migrancy. Even her repeated explanations about the importance of the inside of a vessel, what she often refers to as the void, suggests an intimate understanding of the histories of disenfranchisement and exploitation that have required hidden individual and collective strength to endure.

Odundo's commitment to clay as a universal material rests, in part, on its properties in the hands of creators to produce useful and metaphorical forms that tell stories, hold memories, and connect us. But it also rests on an attentiveness to clay as part of the soil that was divided for profit. Nigerian Canadian artist Oluseye's *Ploughing Liberty* (2021; fig. 28a, 28b) shows a conceptual affinity with a focus on the struggles of Black Loyalists who moved to Nova Scotia after the American Revolution to toil away on rocky, infertile land while the British took arable soil. Oluseye produces minimalist installations through the collection of discarded hockey sticks and antique farm equipment, leaving room for his audiences to consider how popular and everyday items raise broader questions around labour, liberty, and legacies of struggle.

Nearly three decades ago, writing on the occasion of the first major exhibition of African arts at the Guggenheim Museum in New York, critic Michele Wallace cut through all the noise about whether the objects were art, craft, African, or modern to focus on the inexorable linkage between those "stolen" objects and Black bodies. "The fate of African art objects," she remarked, "was not unrelated to the fate of the human bodies also removed from Africa under less-than-ideal circumstances—some of them sold or just handed over and some of them kidnapped." She went on to describe the liminal space inhabited by these objects "stuck on the back-shelves of Western art."[17] Written before the "global turn," Wallace's observations pinpoint the transhistorical, multitemporal parameters of a modern era haunted by the ghosts of the slave trade and colonialism. In Odundo's curatorial interventions in the present exhibition, which may certainly be regarded as contemporary art installations with her pots performing as characters in a criss-crossing spatial-temporal mise-en-scène, she includes us in intimate conversations that free objects, both symbolically and literally, from their dusty shelves and gather the stories of forgotten ancestors.

Notes

1. Emmanuel Cooper, "The Clay of Life: The Ceramic Vessels of Magdalene Odundo," in *Magdalene Odundo*, ed. Anthony Slayter-Ralph (Aldershot: Lund Humphries, 2004), 45.

2. Augustus (Gus) Casely-Hayford, "The Fielding Talk: In Conversation with Magdalene Odundo DBE," Crafts Council, March 1, 2021, https://www.youtube.com /watch?v=uZPfvtFCKNA.

3. Monique Kerman, "Magdalene Odundo," in *Contemporary British Artists of African Descent and the Unburdening of a Generation* (Cham, Switzerland: Palgrave Macmillan by Springer Nature, 2017), 23-56.

4. Stuart Hall, "Black Diaspora Artists in Britain: Three 'Moments' in Post-War History," *History Workshop Journal* 61, no. 1 (March 2006): 10.

5. See Sequoia Miller's chapter in this volume. Also, Simon Olding has noted that Odundo's pots "may take their genesis from the memory of an African marketplace or the deep and rarely seen objects of a specialist museum." Olding, "Magdalene Odundo's *Untitled #10* (1995)," *Journal of Modern Craft* 8, no. 2 (July 2015): 206.

6. Hall, "Black Diaspora Artists in Britain," 5.

7. Ben Enwonwu, "Problems of the African Artist Today," *Présence Africaine*, no. 8–10 (1956): 174–78; Gerard Sekoto, "La responsabilité et la solidarité dans la culture Africaine," *Présence Africaine*, no. 27/28 (1959): 263–67; *Iba Ndiaye: Portrait d'un peintre*, directed by Paulin Soumanou Vieyra (1982; Ballan-Miré, France: PSV Films, 2019); Nancy Dantas, "Tribute and the Modernist Constellations of Bertina Lopes," PostNotes on Art in a Global Context, Museum of Modern Art, New York, November 10, 2021, https:// post.moma.org/tribute-and-the -modernist-constellations-of -bertina-lopes/.

8. Hall, "Black Diaspora Artists in Britain," 53.

9. Magdalene Odundo, "Magdalene Odundo Talks to Linda Theophilus," in *African Metalwork* (London: Crafts Council, 1995), 26.

10. See, for example, Nicholas Bourriaud, *The Altermodern* (London: Tate Publishing, 2009); Hans Belting and Andrea Buddensieg, eds., *The Global Contemporary: Art Worlds after 1989* (Karlsruhe: ZKM Center for Art and Media Karlsruhe, 2011); and Terry Smith, *Contemporary Art: World Currents* (Upper Saddle River, NJ: Prentice Hall, 2011).

11. Terry Smith, "The Contemporaneity Question," in *Antinomies of Art and Culture Modernity, Postmodernity, Contemporaneity*, ed. Terry Smith, Okwui Enwezor, and Nancy Condee (Durham, NC: Duke University Press, 2008), 9; Mark Augé, *An Anthropology for Contemporaneous Worlds* (Stanford, CA: Stanford University Press, 1999), 89; Nicolas Bourriaud, *Altermodern* (London: Tate Publishing, 2009); David Joselit, *Heritage and Debt: Art in Globalization* (Cambridge, MA: MIT Press, 2020).

12. Belting and Buddensieg, eds.,"Introduction," in *The Global Contemporary*, 6–7.

13. Hal Foster, "Questionnaire on 'The Contemporary,'" *October*, no. 130 (Fall 2009): 3.

14. John Picton, "Africa and a Potter's Art," in *Magdalene Odundo*, ed. Y. Joris ('s-Hertogenbosch, Netherlands: Museum Het Kruithuis, 1994), 37.

15. *Magdalene Odundo: The Journey of Things*, Hepworth Wakefield, Yorkshire, February 16–June 2, 2019, https:// hepworthwakefield.org/whats-on /magdalene-odundo-the-journey -of-things/.

16. Sally Frater, quoted in Alex Greenberger, "Denyse Thomasos Finds Life after Death as a Canadian Retrospective Leads to a Posthumous Rise," *Art News*, February 7, 2023, https://www .artnews.com/art-news/artists/denyse -thomasos-retrospective-whitney -biennial-paintings-1234656408/. See also Adrienne Edwards, "My Artist Ghost," *New York Times*, March 23, 2022, https://www.nytimes.com/2022/03/23 /arts/design/denyse-thomasos-whitney -biennial.html.

17. Michele Wallace, "The Prison House of Culture: Why African Art? Why the Guggenheim? Why Now?," *Black Renaissance* 1, no. 2 (Fall 1997): 167.

Fig. 29 Magdalene Odundo, *Untitled*, 1997. Ceramic, 36 × 43 × 43 cm. Maxine and Stuart Frankel Foundation for Art

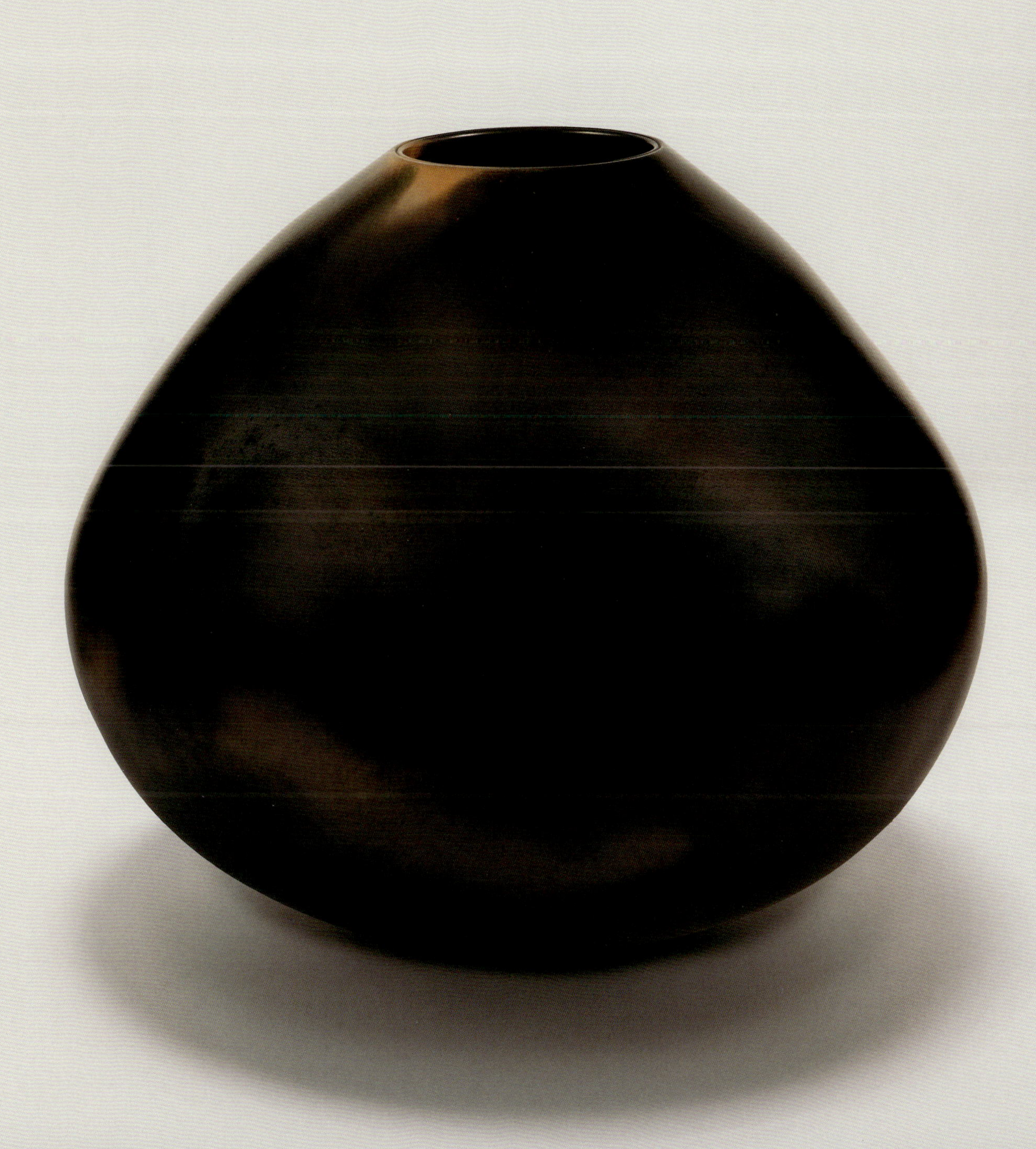

Fig. 30 Magdalene Odundo, *Untitled*,
2009. Ceramic, 43 × 36 × 36 cm

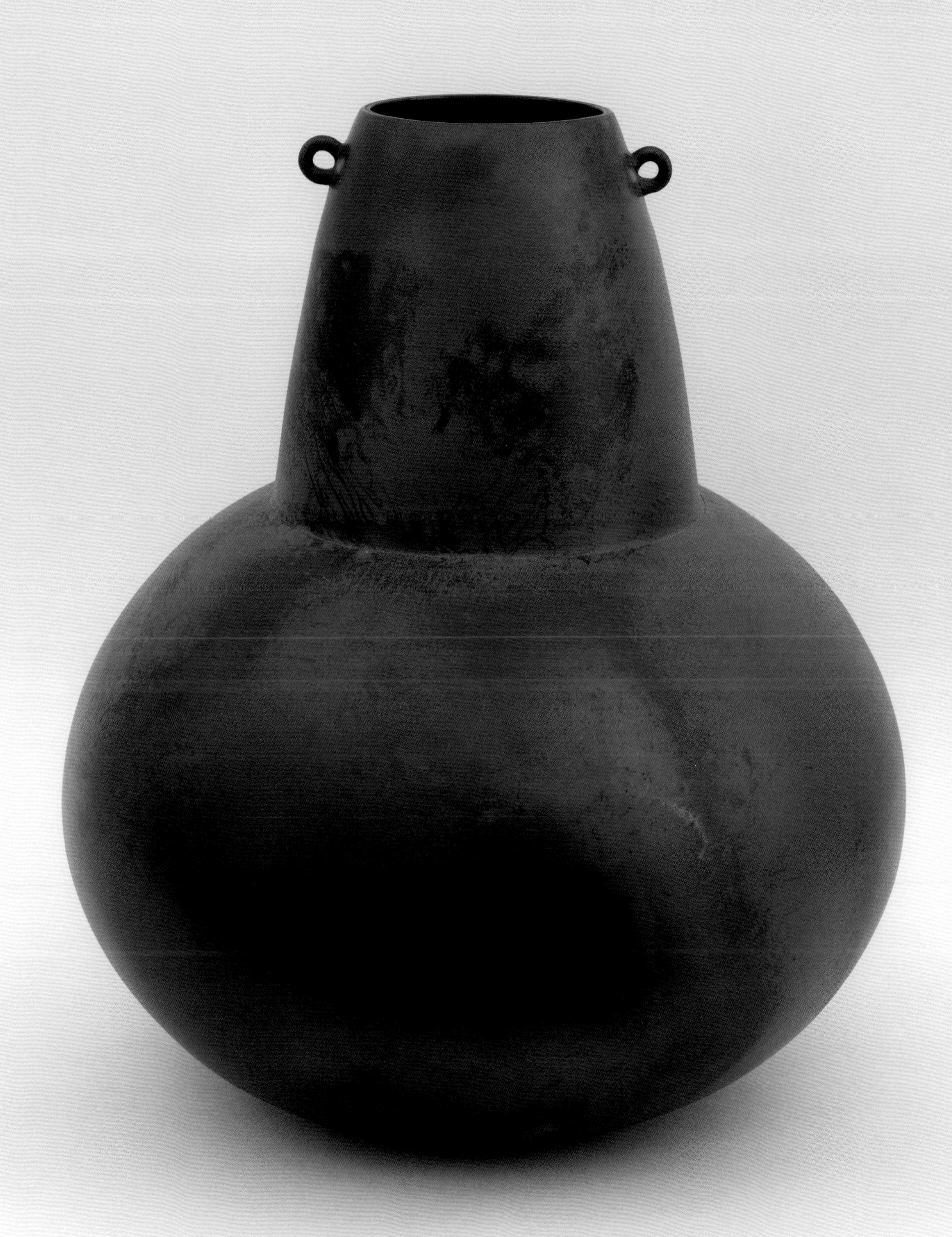

Fig. 31 Magdalene Odundo, *Untitled*,
1987. Ceramic, 37 × 22 × 22 cm. Maxine
and Stuart Frankel Foundation for Art

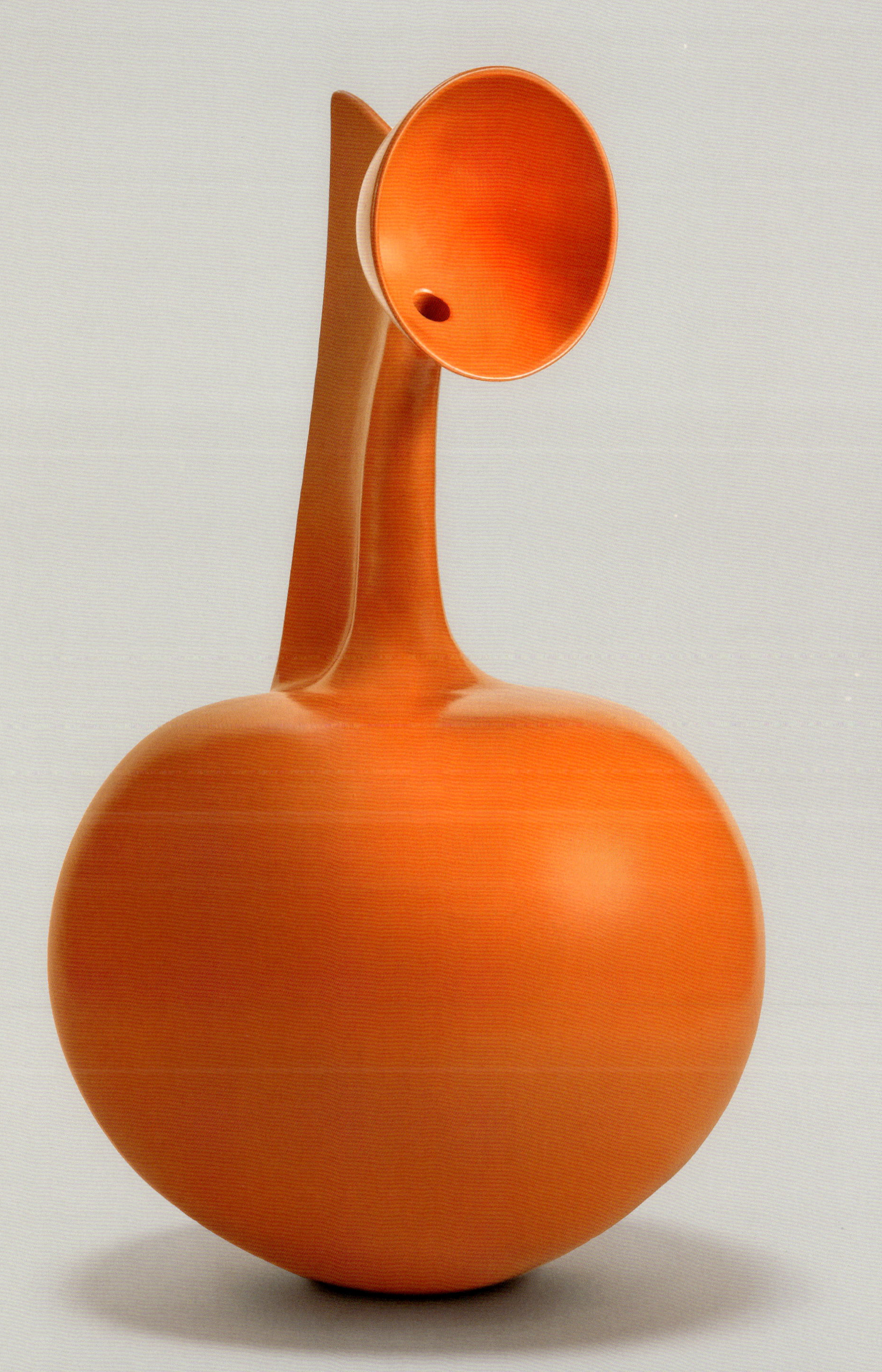

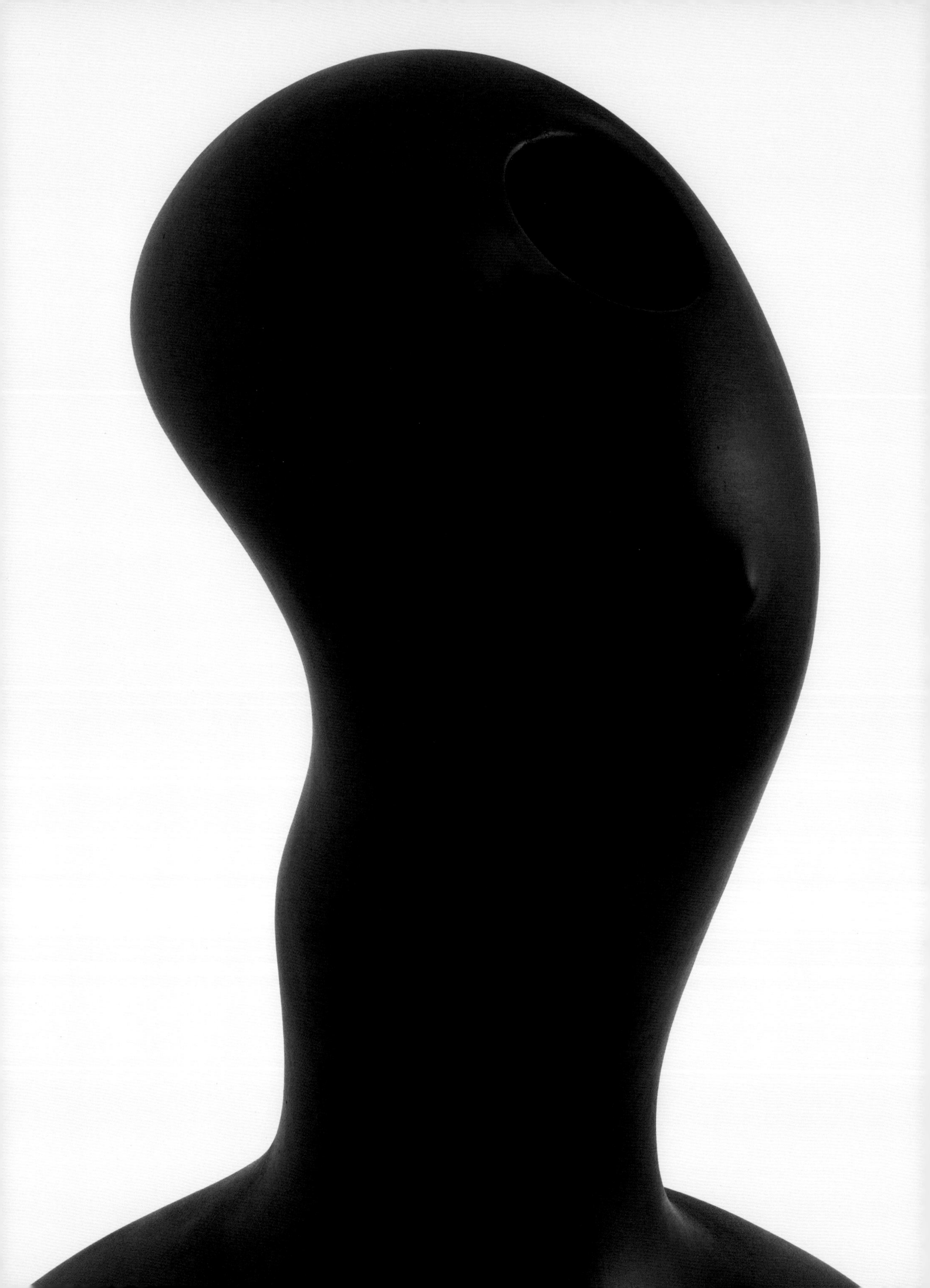

Nehal El-Hadi

A Smooth Hybridity
Magdalene Odundo's Dancing Vessels

You don't just have an idea, cast something, or allow some-thing to set, and it keeps its form. With clay, there is this constant potential for movement—even after the firing process.[1]

—Phoebe Collings-James

The black dancing body is the existential body.[2]
—Brenda Dixon Gottschild

Magdalene Odundo's vessels are material presentations of braided temporalities comprising various pasts—her own history, ancestral memory, material memory—and presents. They traverse geographies of being, making, and understanding; the labour of Black women that produces the aesthetics of African cultures; and the colonial journeys of objects, makers, and interpretations. Odundo's works are beautiful, and as Christina Sharpe reminds us, "Beauty is a practice…beauty is a method."[3] In the vessels produced by Odundo's determined pursuit of ideal form, beauty is a reminder, a grounding, and a transcendental pleasure.

Odundo begins her creative process by understanding what the interior space of the vessel needs to be, shaping it in collaboration with both the clay and her understanding of the shape it should possess, which is possibly determined by ancestral-memory. Odundo was born and raised in Kenya and apprenticed in Nairobi as a graphic designer before relocating to England, where she

Fig. 33 Magdalene Odundo, *Untitled*, 1995. Ceramic, 51 × 29 × 29 cm. Maxine and Stuart Frankel Foundation for Art

transferred her focus to clay. As an undergraduate student she later travelled to Nigeria, where she was taught by Ladi Kwali and Lami Toto, among others. There, she discovered that ceramics was about learning to work *with* clay: "The process of hand building with clay is fused with sound and bodily movement. That leads to an awareness of the form and shape you are making."[4]

The connections and associations that we make between an object, its function, and its history reflect not only who we are but also our desires and needs, and our perceived absences. Odundo's sculptures remind me of where I'm from in two distinct ways. The first is in their resemblance to vessels from my homeland of Sudan, specifically the coffeepots known as *jebena*, originally from Ethiopia, and the clay water containers called zeer; these references hint at their original purposes, serving as an aide-mémoire to diasporic recollections. Second, in the gestures of Odundo's vessels, I see body movements associated with traditional East African dances. While Odundo was influenced by the graceful movements of ballet dancers, these gestures in the context of her forms appear closer to East African dances. In Odundo's work, these dance characteristics are noticed, extended, and extrapolated.

Clay is an abundant material in Khartoum, sourced from the banks of the Nile. Houses are built from bricks prepared simply by shaping the mud and allowing it to dry. Functional ceramic dishware and vessels are ubiquitous, made using traditional techniques that have remained mostly unchanged over time. Jebena pots, used to brew spiced coffee, are smooth vessels with curvaceously rounded bottoms, long-necked spouts, and handles thickened to protect the handler from the heat (fig. 32). Unglazed, they are often burnished with a spoon to produce a shiny, smooth finish. Some have colourful patterns with painted pointillistic accents or engraved geometric figures, in deference to more modern design sensibilities. In my home in Toronto, I make coffee using a moka pot, carefully adding a traditional spice mixture of dried cardamom pods, star anise, and cinnamon bark to the ground grains. I don't own a jebena; as an object, it is an artefact of a cultural practice I don't participate in for practical reasons (the coffee is brewed over hot coals) and historical ones (I hadn't been taught how to make coffee in this manner).

Odundo's smoothly rounded vessels extend features of jebena pots into more dynamic manifestations. Her forms imply the vernacular of East African vessels in their suggestions of lugs or handles and exaggerated mouths and shoulders. Encountering a jebena-like vessel on display in a gallery space, albeit at a larger scale, is a dislocative experience, the context making the familiar strange. The more amphora-like vessels provoke another recall, that of vessels that make use of clay as a refrigerating material.

Zeer, water-filled unglazed vessels, were once common sights on the sandy city streets in Khartoum

Fig. 32 Unknown artist, *Jebena*, undated. Earthenware, 20.3 × 14 cm. Siddig el Nigoumi's Collection

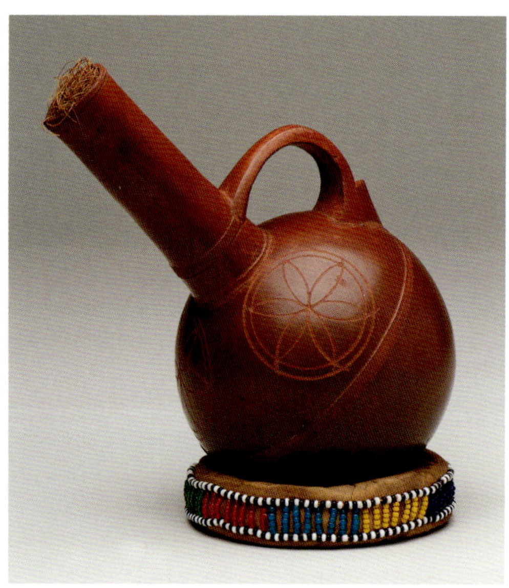

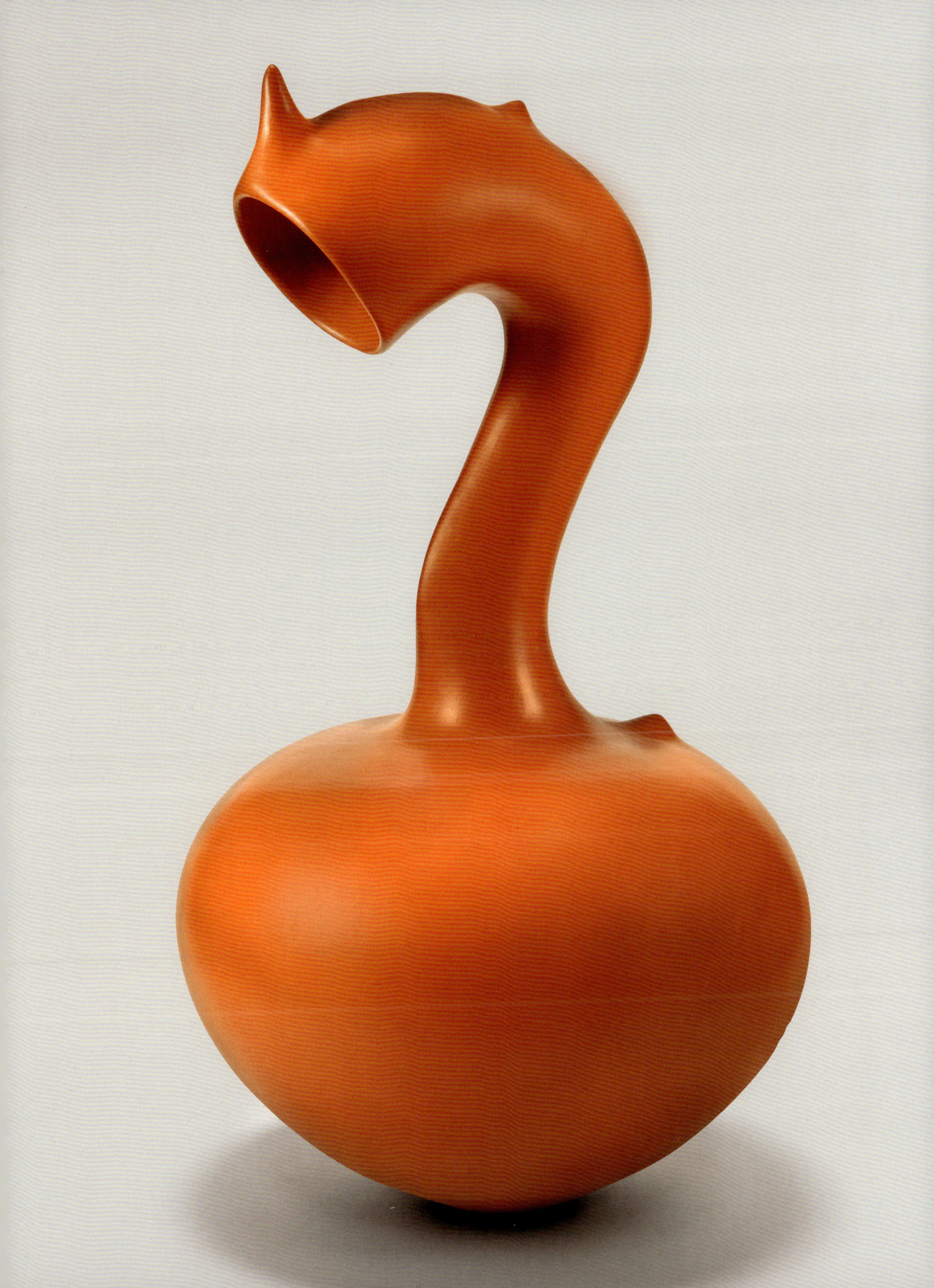

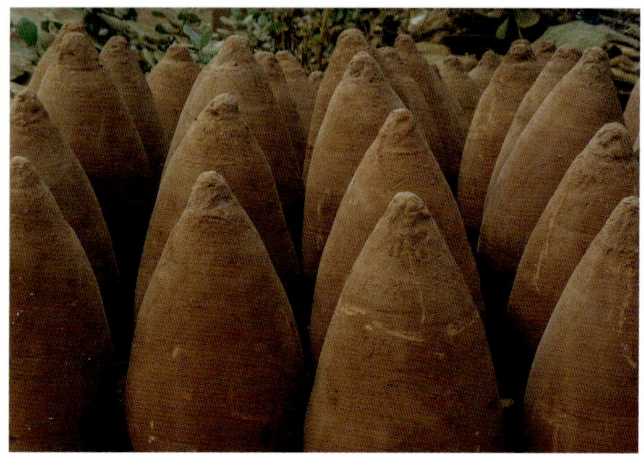

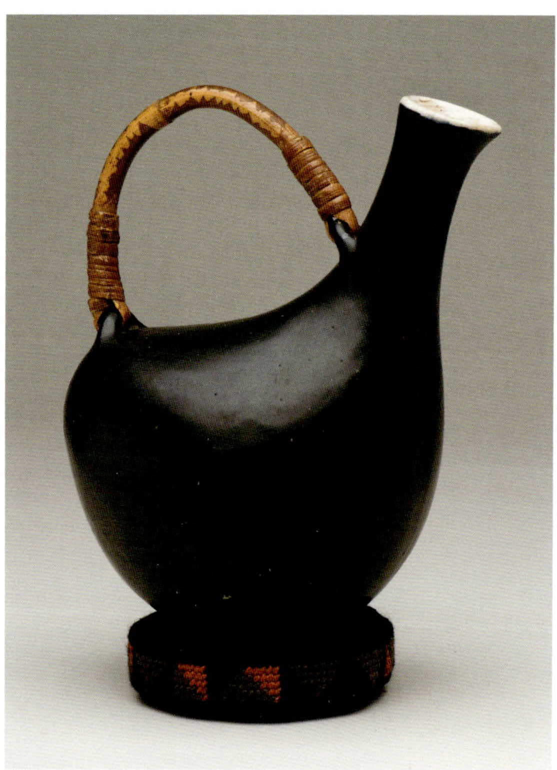

(fig. 34), before war broke out in the city. Left outside houses in a gesture of generosity to passers-by, these large clay pots contained cool water available for anyone to quench their thirst. Undecorated and amphora-like, with conical bottoms and suspended on a frame, they have a beauty that lies in their simple form and contents—the gift of water in one of the hottest cities on Earth. In Sudan and throughout sub-Saharan Africa, clay, in its design and as material, is employed as a technology to keep the water cool.

In markets in Khartoum, shops once displayed rows upon rows of identical jebena, zeer, and other clay products. Their hand-produced uniformity reflected a deep body memory of techniques and processes that repeatedly re-created these vessels at different scales.

In addition to her encounters with similar vessels in Kenya, Odundo worked and exhibited in England with Sudanese ceramicist Siddig el Nigoumi, whom she considered a teacher, an elder, and an influence.[5] El Nigoumi was loosely affiliated with the Khartoum school, a modernist art movement founded in the mid-twentieth century by such renowned Sudanese artists as the painters Kamala Ibrahim Ishag and Ibrahim El Salahi. A proponent of drawing from one's own culture and heritage, el Nigoumi's work was nevertheless influenced by Japanese and European ceramics. His own mimetic vessels invited a consideration of the jebena's elegant form—its proportions, curves, and smoothness—as well as its function (fig. 35). After el Nigoumi left Sudan to live in Farnham, he began referencing his Sudanese culture intensively, developing firing techniques to create the same effects and introducing historical Nubian graphic elements alongside disparate British iconographies such as crossword patterns.

Like el Nigoumi's work, Odundo's practice is built on a foundation of traditional processes and African pottery techniques, including hand building and burnishing pieces to a high polish. While honouring these traditions, Odundo further extrapolates her object references, isolating and exaggerating feature elements of jebena and other clay vessels to produce more idealized representations of their form.

"On the one hand," writes Egyptologist Giulia d'Ercole, "a pot is an object of daily use, relatively simple in form and very tangible. On the other hand, even an ordinary vessel concentrates human creativity, technological awareness, and social complexity."[6] Rather than eschewing traditional practices or avoiding the everyday in her cultural references, Odundo examines the historicity of ceramic practice in a close study of form and how form carries and conveys meaning. The poet Elizabeth Alexander defines the Black interior as "a metaphysical space," where we can "envision what we are not meant to envision: complex black selves, real and enactable black power, rampant and unfetishized black beauty."[7] The interiors of Odundo's vessels, shaped by hand, become repositories for Black interiorities, memories, and cultural practices; their hybridized exteriors reference traditional earthenware forms rendered in such a manner as to make their beauty indisputable.

The accessibility of clay and its malleability makes it, as curator Jareh Das describes, "a time-based medium offering a range of transformative possibilities [that] are explorations of cyborg futures, fragmented forms, the body as conceptual, fluid, full of contradictions and slippages."[8] Here, I am drawn to the anthropomorphic qualities of Odundo's sculptures and her references to dancers paused in the moment of a movement. Her extrapolations of form and intention power the sensuality of her sculptures. A curve suggests a smile or a shoulder; the rounded proportions, a belly or a bottom. Other aspects evoke an elongated neck, a bony protrusion, a folded crevice, a fat jiggle. Her vessels are often described as being sinuous, voluptuous, seductive, and curvaceous, and these qualities magnify the relationship between the human body and clay, between movement and sculpture.

"Attitudes, or positions of the body, as realized in African sculpture, often betray choreographic implications," writes historian Robert Farris Thompson in his call for a consideration of motion when reflecting upon African art.[9] In Odundo's Asymmetrical Series, in particular, the vessels' postures and poses reference a familiar choreographic vocabulary. Brenda Dixon Gottschild, writing on the Black body in dance, describes:

> Like the ordinary/extraordinary of the black dancing body, traditional African dance utilizes the ordinary imagery of home and community (whether mortar, pestle, scythe, animal imagery, or moral tenets of good and evil) to reach for the extraordinary—those ineffable flights that can be expressed only in the medium of the dancing body and are not necessarily translatable into words or the verbal telling of a story. The real story in African dance is the manifestation and presence of the dancing body. It doesn't mean something else: It is what it is![10]

With their apparently flawless surfaces and gravity-defying postures, Odundo's Asymmetrical Series works, while not explicitly sculptures of the human body, seem to be caught in a moment and/or a movement. The kinesics are reminiscent of Hadendoa neck-craning dances, Ethiopian eskista, or Kenyan chakacha (fig. 33), and I understand Odundo herself to be a vessel and a conduit for movement memory in producing these gestures.

Philosopher Denise Ferreira da Silva, in response to a photograph of the artist Simone Leigh working on her 2019 sculpture
Brick House, writes:

> A thinking that refigures the doings of black women
> approaches the intellectual and the creative (or the critical
> + creative, as I have been thinking about it for a while now)
> always in reference to a mode of existing (as a condition of
> the world and not as the condition of being in the world, I
> repeat) that yields that which is at once a feat, a deed, a
> burden, and artifact.[11]

This proposition that doing—or making—by Black women yields
"a feat, a deed, a burden, and artifact," when applied to Odundo's
sculptures, creates a generative referential framework through
which to understand her vessels.

For Black artists, Odundo has a special standing. The Brooklyn-
based Sudanese Somali artist Dina Nur Satti, for example, speaks
of the inspiration she finds in Odundo's work and example: "It's so
rare as a woman from Africa to find role models and elders who
so beautifully connect indigenous craft methods and the modern
design world."[12] Odundo's experience and work also serve to
highlight the connection between Indigenous and African matrilineal pottery traditions, which, as Kym E. Young notes, have "been
socially and ethnically ingrained in these cultures as a women's art;
and the processes of extracting clay from the earth, formation of
vessels, and decoration of finished works bears striking similarities
between the two vastly separated cultures."[13]

Leigh is outspoken in her dedication to Black women as both
audience and focus of her work. As art critic Siddhartha Mitter
stated: "These interests stoke a core concern of her art practice:
Black female subjectivity—the sense of self of Black women in the
world, their histories, their work, their inner lives."[14] I find this "core
concern" with Black womanhood and our histories, bodies, and
production also present in Odundo's work. This dedication to and
reflection of Black womanhood, explicitly stated in Leigh's work, is
implicitly read in Odundo's expression of forms and choice of
techniques. Odundo's focus on Black women's representation and
labour serves to disrupt the hegemonic norms of art institutions, and
her dancing vessels invite Black women to celebrate our presence.

These associations and their implications underlie the viewing
experience of Odundo's art: in her work's aestheticism and elevation
of form lies a foundation in the labour and value of Black women. Her
dancer-vessels are a synthesis of the artist's travels, education,
knowledges, experience, and role as a conduit. They are hybridized
and collated presentations of traditional knowledge and colonial
passages, elevated in status and stature.

And before all, they are beautiful.

Notes

1. Jareh Das, Phoebe Collings-James, and Julia Phillips, "How Clay Is Connected to Our Bodies," *Frieze*, no. 223 (November/December 2021), https://www.frieze.com/article/how-clay-connected-our-bodies.

2. Brenda Dixon Gottschild, *The Black Dancing Body: A Geography from Coon to Cool* (New York: Palgrave Macmillan, 2016), 15.

3. Christina Sharpe, "Note 51: Beauty Is a Method," in *Ordinary Notes* (Toronto: Alfred A. Knopf, 2023), 80.

4. Magdalene Odundo, "How Travel Transformed Magdalene Odundo's Ceramics Practice," *Frieze*, no. 223 (November/December 2021), https://www.frieze.com/article/how-travel-transformed-magdalene-odundos-ceramics-practice.

5. Sebastian Blackie, "Cultural Reflections: Review of Magdalene Odundo at Cambridge," *Ceramic Review*, no. 324 (November/December 2023), https://www.ceramicreview.com/articles/cultural-reflections/.

6. Giulia D'Ercole, "Seventy Years of Pottery Studies in the Archaeology of Mesolithic and Neolithic Sudan," *African Archaeological Review* 38, no. 2 (2021): 345–72.

7. Elizabeth Alexander, *The Black Interior* (Saint Paul, MN: Graywolf Press, 2004), x.

8. Jareh Das, "Performative Clay," *Mater Digital*, https://mater.digital/chapterone/jareh-das/.

9. Robert Farris Thompson, *African Art in Motion: Icon and Act* (Washington, DC: National Gallery of Art, 5.

10. Gottschild, *The Black Dancing Body*, 15.

11. Denise Ferreira da Silva, "How," *e-flux Journal*, no. 105 (December 2019), https://www.e-flux.com/journal/105/305515/how/.

12. "The Queue: Dina Nur Satti," American Craft Council (blog), October 4, 2021, https://www.craftcouncil.org/post/queue-dina-nur-satti.

13. Kym E. Young, "Matriarchal Heritages in Women's Pottery: An Examination of Similarities in West African and Native American Women's Pottery Traditions," *McNair Scholars Journal of the University of Wisconsin-Superior* 3 (2002): 26.

14. Siddhartha Mitter, "Simone Leigh, in the World," *New York Times*, April 14, 2022, https://www.nytimes.com/2022/04/14/arts/design/simone-leigh-venice-biennale-us-pavilion.html.

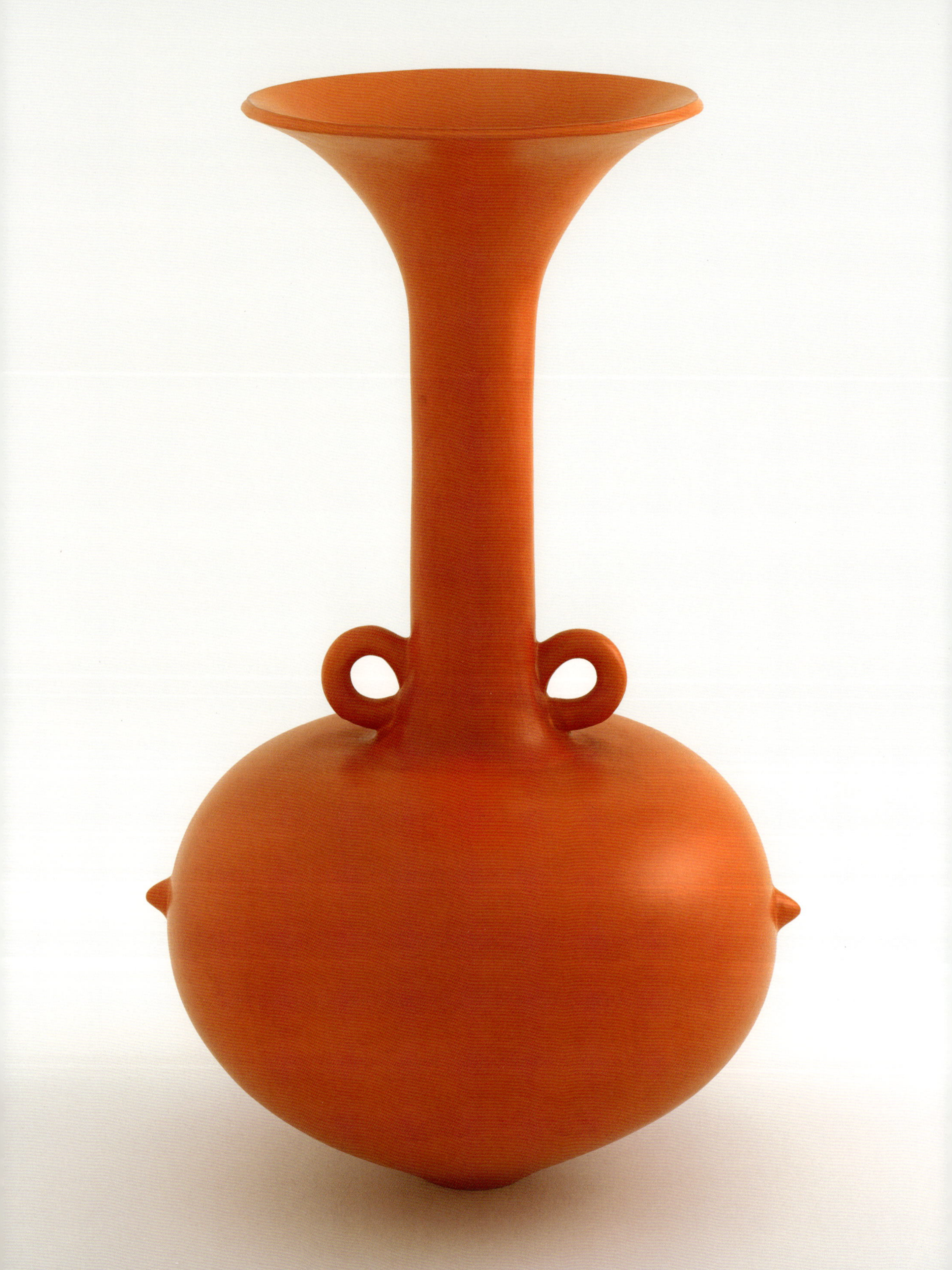

Fig. 36 Magdalene Odundo, *Untitled*,
2020. Ceramic, 56 × 36 × 33 cm

Fig. 37 Magdalene Odundo, *Untitled*,
1995. Ceramic, 43.2 × 28 × 28 cm. Yale
University Art Gallery

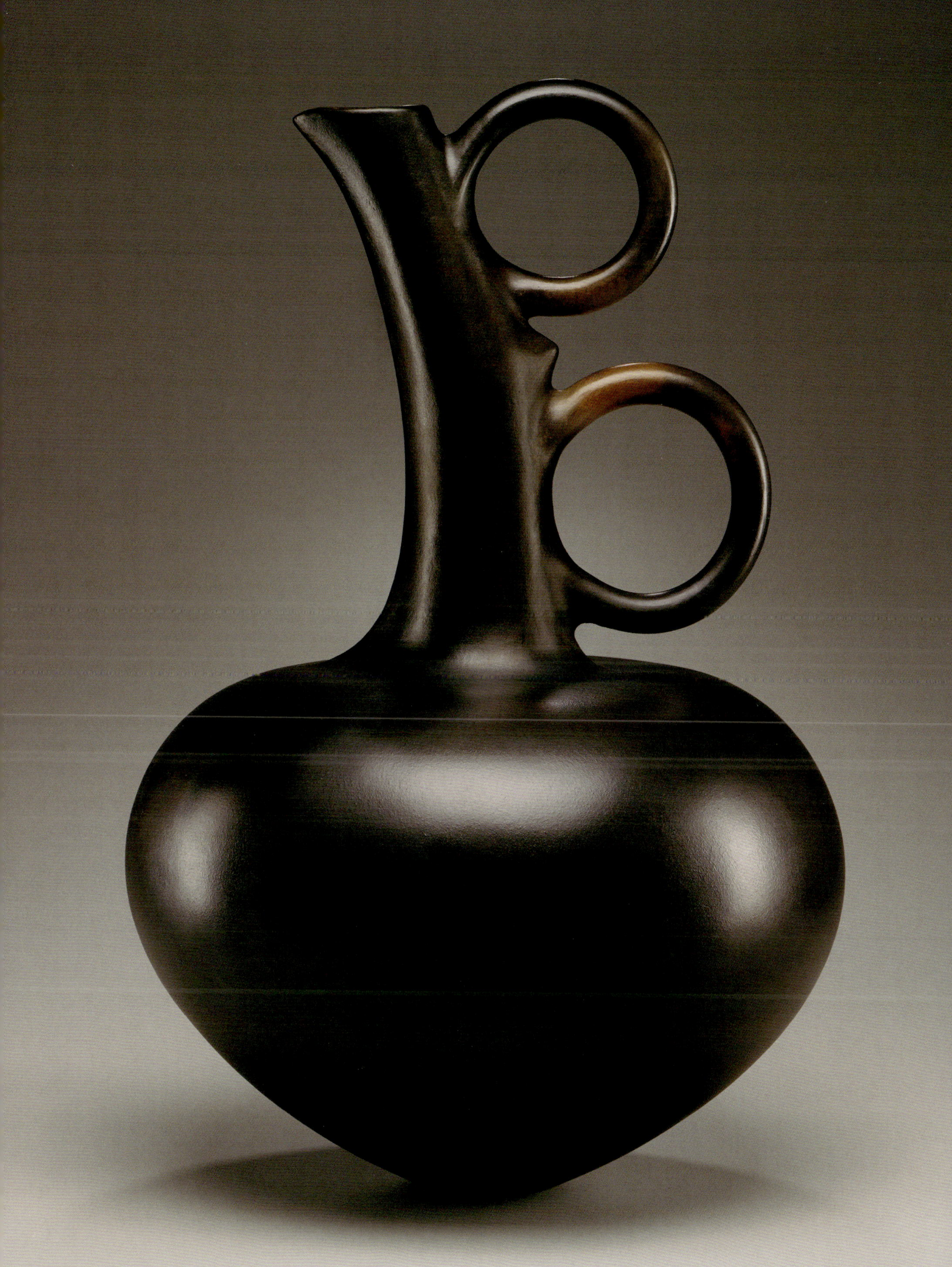

SM While there are many places we could begin, I'd like to start by asking to what extent your pieces embody or have a narrative.

MO I hope they are telling a story, it is very important to me that objects have a narrative. The works speak about me, my siblings, and my people. The more we decipher objects, the more they tell us about the people who made and used them. Hopefully, a hundred years from now somebody will know what I was trying to say in my work and what my world was about. I feel I am able to express in my work a narrative about who I am as a person, while also not telling everything.

SM Could you say more about that balance of telling and not telling? Have you always had a sense of where that balance lies?

MO From a young age, I had this sense of revealing and not revealing. Growing up on the coast of Kenya, I liked the fact that storytelling was generally in the form of riddles. Those riddles formed the basis of cultural teaching, ways of disseminating knowledge, and telling our history. To solve the riddle was to understand the story. This approach has informed my work, which I hope offers the viewer space to find their own stories.

SM Your pieces do have a sense of being riddles, in that you give us clues but we have to find our own path through them, to the interior.

MO My pieces engage with this notion of containment, balancing the contained and uncontained. The outer shell protects the inner aspect of the work, and the outside form leads you to want to know what the inside is all about. The ceramic is the wall that divides these two perspectives or worlds. The human body is like that as well, we have this wonderful outer skin that conceals all that is within.

SM The interiors of your works strike me as very quiet spaces. You once mentioned to me that a lot of your work over the years has sought to create a space for silence. I'm curious how this idea of silence relates to the notion of concealing or not telling.

MO It is important for me that when people are viewing my work they have a moment of quiet that enables them to navigate between what they see and what they feel. They need that moment of silence to experience the wonderment that one wants, to be amazed or astonished, creating a sensation that leads to philosophical reflection on what the work is all about.

SM While there is quietude in your work, it also embodies a certain drama or flair. Would you say there's humour or sassiness in your work?

MO Well, there's an element of wanting the piece to attract dialogue, to attract comment. There's a humour about some of the work alongside the seriousness. The humor helps evoke the fuller experience of being human, wanting to dance as well as reflect on our emotions.

SM How do you think about mark making in your work?

MO I make marks and then erase them, because the marks are like a template for the forms. Through erasing the marks I am working towards simplifying the profile of the vessel and seeking clarity. The time I spend creating the lines and edges of the work is like drawing on a three-dimensional piece.

SM How did traditional models for learning intersect for you with formal education?

MO My primary and secondary school education in Kenya was based on the British colonial system. I took O-level and A-level exams that were in preparation for university admission. The only traditional learning I had was through contact made when visiting relatives in western Kenya. The latter was to become very important when I was seeking to find out who I was outside the colonial paradigm. We all had to navigate these contrasting traditions through language—speaking our own languages in rural areas with our relatives. When we got back to school in the city, we were allowed to speak only English. By the time I was at university in the UK, I had philosophically accepted that I was always going to negotiate my life between these two forms of learning. And that duality remains today. So there is part of me that appreciates the value of learning from masters within apprenticeships—from watching and observing—and another part, that which involves taking notes, drawing, and listening. One is practical, the other is theoretical.

SM Have you carried those dual ways of learning into your teaching over the years?

MO I was very much a practical, hands-on teacher. I was on the shop floor, as it were, working with the students on experience-based learning and teaching. Theory would come from discussing books and journals in tutorials. I would always emphasize the advantages of reading, research, and using libraries and museums as sources of information. I hoped that my students were able to use that practice in their own work.

SM How did Kenya's struggle for independence impact you growing up?

MO Kenya gained independence in 1963 and it was a powerful moment for us all. The mood was very optimistic. In the 1960s, we were very aware of other liberation movements, including the Black power movement, anti-apartheid, and others. The influence of music from the US was growing amongst the youth. What is very interesting is that we were all very knowledgeable about international current affairs. Those movements educated us and allowed me to find a way of expression through the work I was doing. By the time I came to England, those ideas had been cemented in my mind.

SM Did you think of yourself as political at that time?

MO I'm not sure I ever thought of myself as political, although I did think of myself as part of those movements. By the time I went to university, I realized just how much the colonial system had become embedded within our political system and our thinking. There was much optimism at the time because many former colonies were gaining independence, and it was exciting to be part of that.

SM Could you reflect on arriving in the UK from Kenya and seeing work by Western artists who had drawn from African objects, some which may have been familiar from your own experiences?

MO Well, at first, I was very pleased to note they were inspired by African art. It elevated my pride in the fact that the art that I was being told was "primitive" when I was in Kenya was being celebrated by contemporary artists. Then I became interested in why the works by African artists were always labeled anonymous and yet they had made such an impact on Western artists. I knew that these pieces had been made in connection with rituals and ceremonies. The appropriation by these artists missed the spiritual dimension embedded in these works. They described it as "abstract art," which only meant that it was not pictorial. There's a lot of meaning—majesty—within the pieces that were removed from their cultures of origin during colonial times.

It became important for me to connect these pieces to their rightful cultural provenance, so I became interested in how anthropology, archaeology, ethnography, and museum studies were being taught. I was able to situate the pieces historically and that became a way of expressing myself within the practice of making objects. Making vessels, closed or open, became a spiritual quest for me in trying to manifest all these concepts into the artworks.

SM How does your sense of belonging with your ancestral community in Kenya balance with your sense of belonging in, say, the university or Farnham?

MO When I'm back in Kenya where I grew up, I don't feel as if I have left. Although things have changed materially, my people are in many ways the same as they were, full of aspiration and hope. I have worked to retain my cultural heritage through language, even though I identify with Farnham as well. Farnham is a great community, full of artists and interesting people, but I think of Kenya as home.

SM You have had several exhibitions in Kenya. How did it feel to show your work there? Did you find the response similar to that in the West?

MO I have had several exhibitions in Kenya that were important for me, one in 1985 during the Women's Decade Conference and a solo exhibition at the British Council in Nairobi in 2004. These were both very successful, and I especially found support amongst younger artists. The appreciation of my work by my relatives and other contemporary Kenyan artists was very meaningful. What was especially pleasing to me was the reaction to my work was the same as in the West.

SM Has your way of thinking about spirituality changed over the years?

MO I am not sure this has changed. Working with clay is a practice for me but also a spiritual connection with who I am. I am still exploring that notion of a vernacular shelter within the pieces I make. There's a potency to the inside of them. They are where I go and hide. I feel there's a sacredness, especially the interiors of the work. I still concentrate on making the interiors as perfect as the exteriors. I believe that one's being is determined by that which is not seen, on the inside. The interiors engender curiosity. And, ultimately, that's how we approach each other as human beings. I hope my pieces fly off the pedestal, so to speak, and gesture towards the heavens. I hope they enable people to reach beyond simply looking at the form.

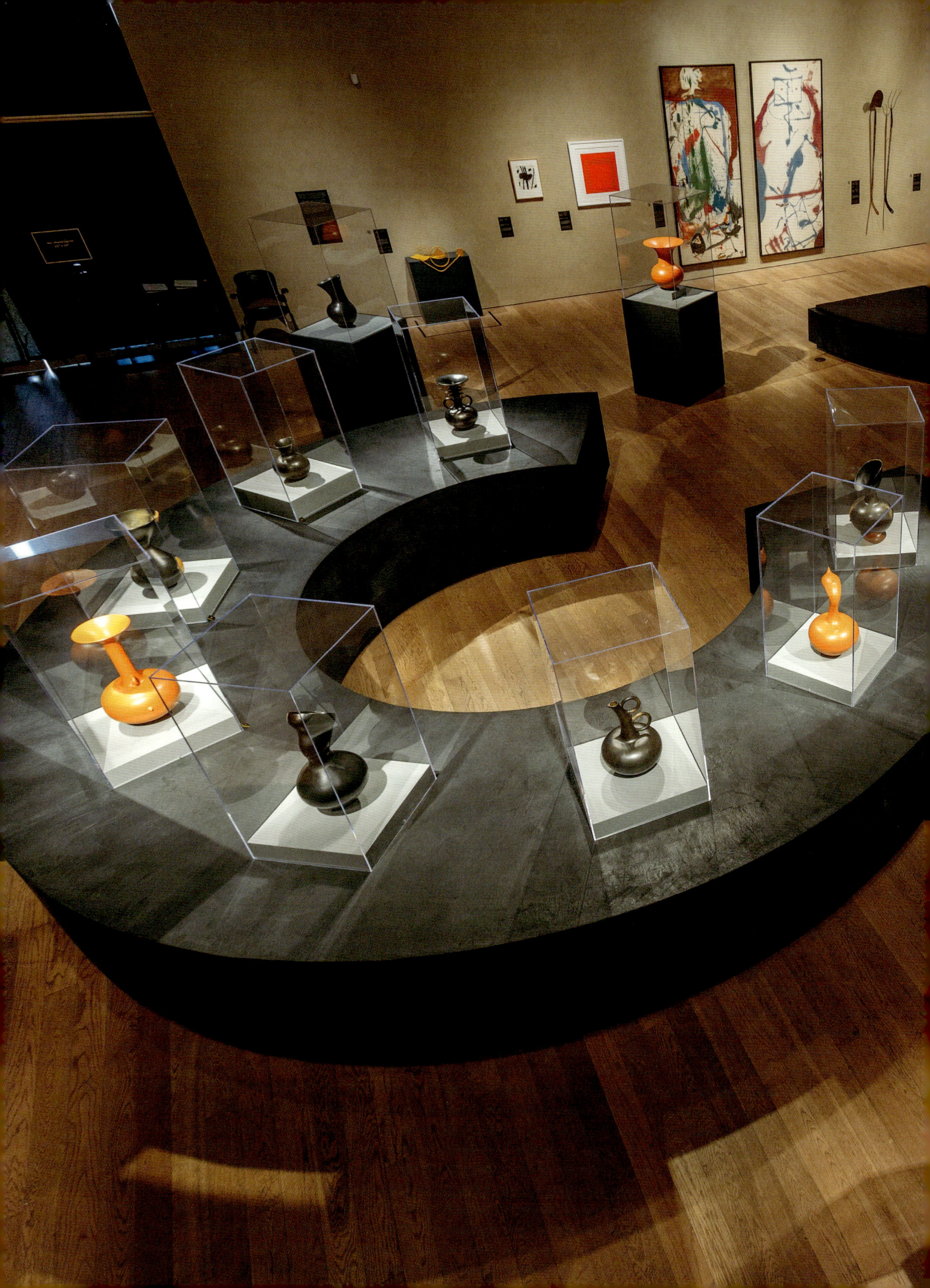

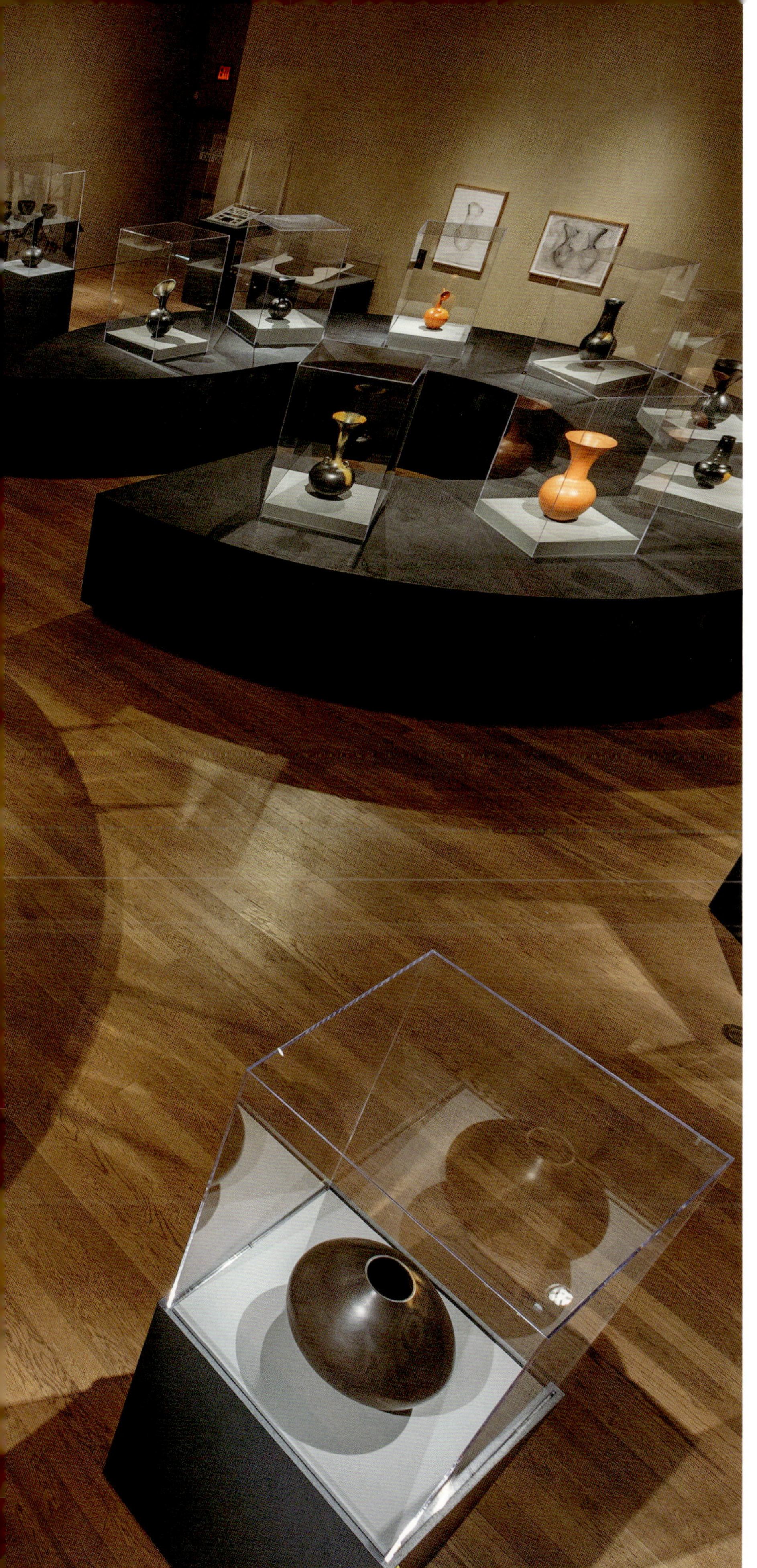

Fig. 38 View of *Magdalene Odundo: A Dialogue with Objects* exhibition, held at the Gardiner Museum, 2023–2024

Sequoia Miller

Prints and Drawings

Magdalene Odundo studied drawing and printmaking alongside ceramics in art school and has maintained both disciplines within her studio practice. She often draws in tandem to working in clay, advancing the drawing and ceramic form together, or rendering a vessel after it is made. Her drawn vessels function individually, but also as groups, almost as if they are speaking to one another.

Odundo's figural prints reveal her study of the human body, often spontaneous and gestural. We see the artist exploring and responding to the transitions in the figure, as well as shifts in weight and balance. The works on paper form a link between Odundo's perception of the figure and her ceramic vessels, which abstract the human reference and synthesize it with other resonant forms. We see how mark making on paper, lithography stone, and metal plate translate into the highly controlled rims, profiles, and protuberances on her ceramics.

Prints and ceramics also share a material sensibility, both requiring focused manual working as well as a sense of handing the work over to the press or kiln to complete.

Spontaneous, directly figural, and often inspired from daily life, Odundo's two-dimensional works on paper reveal the depth and complexity of the artist's practice.

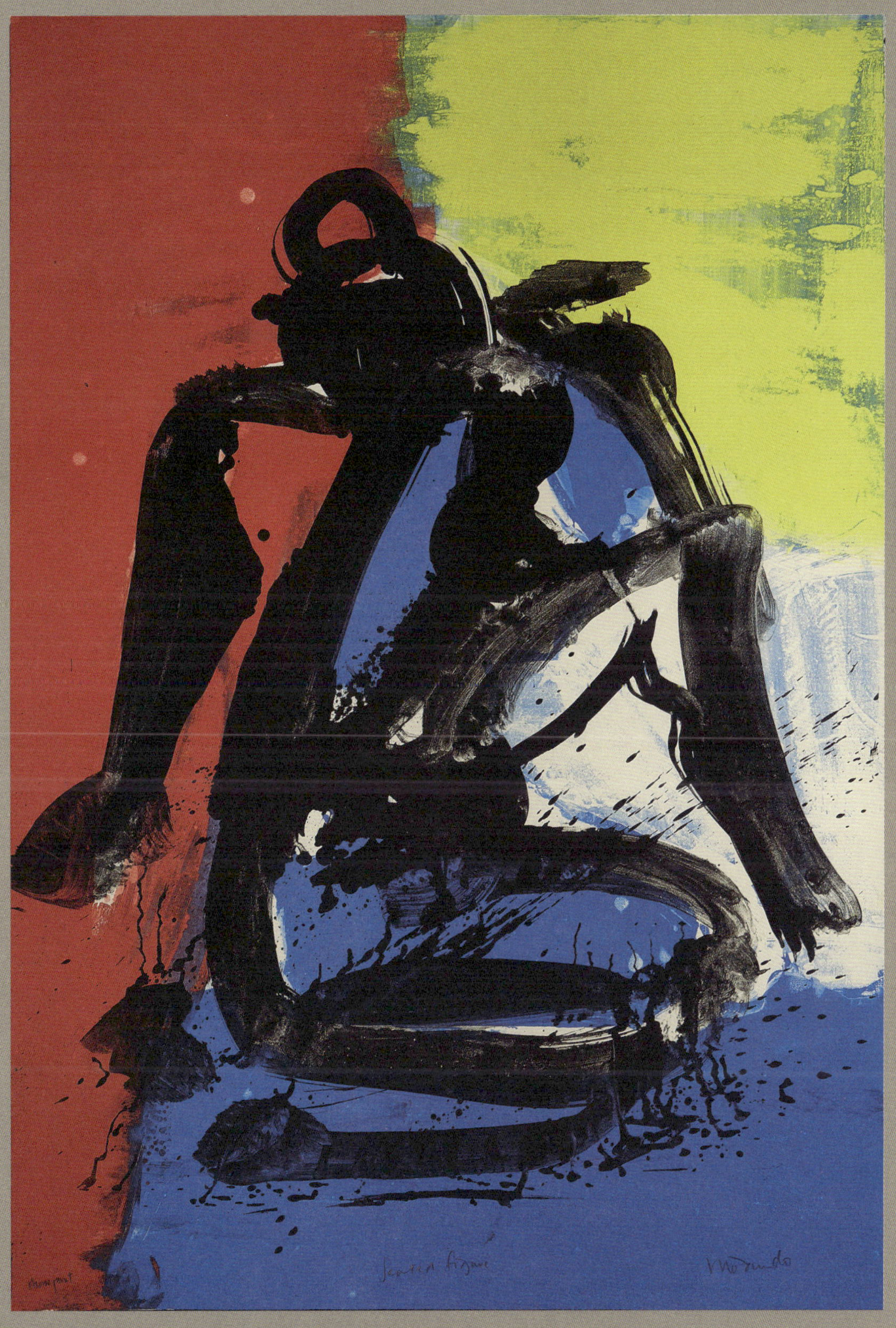
monoprint
Seated figure
Morundo

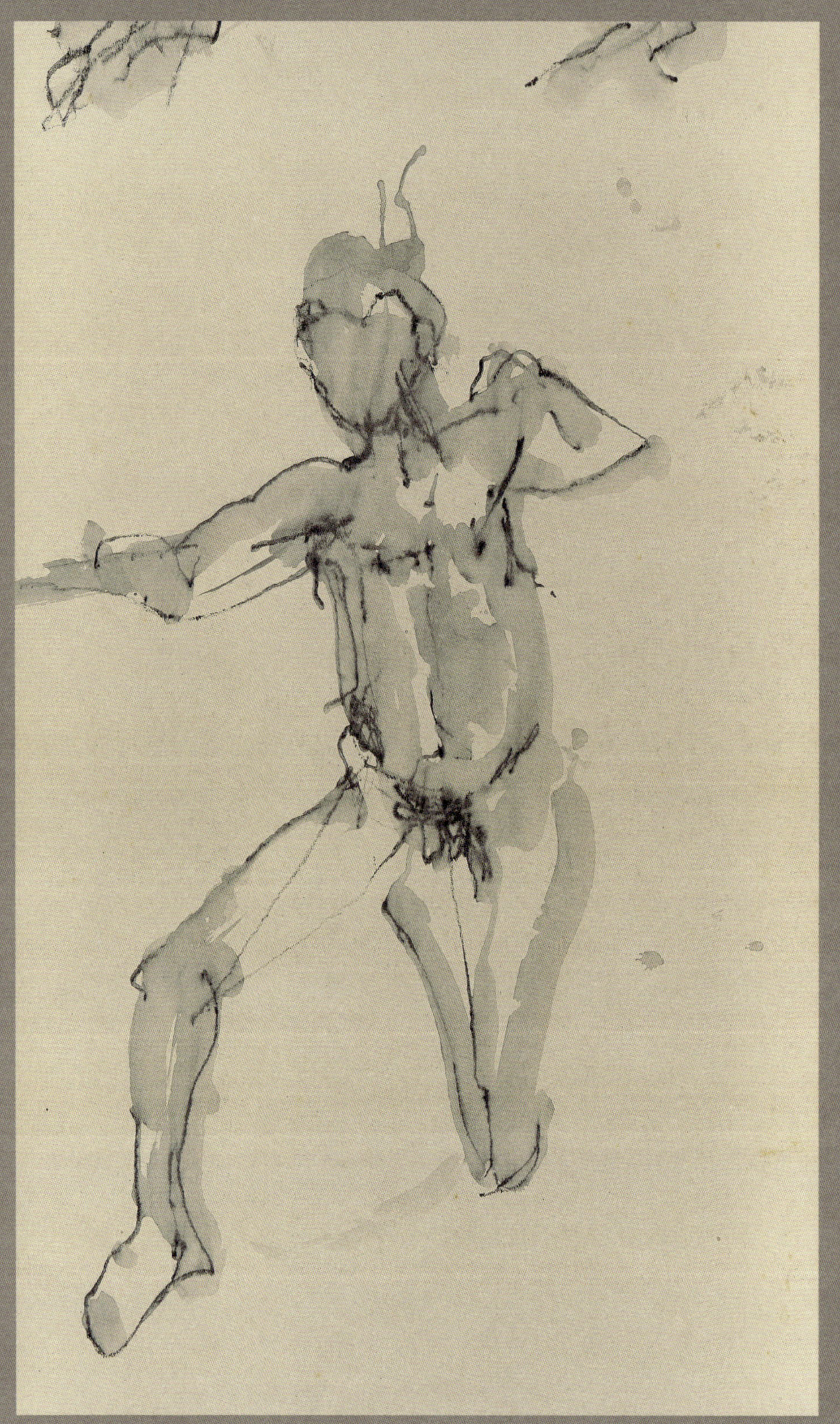

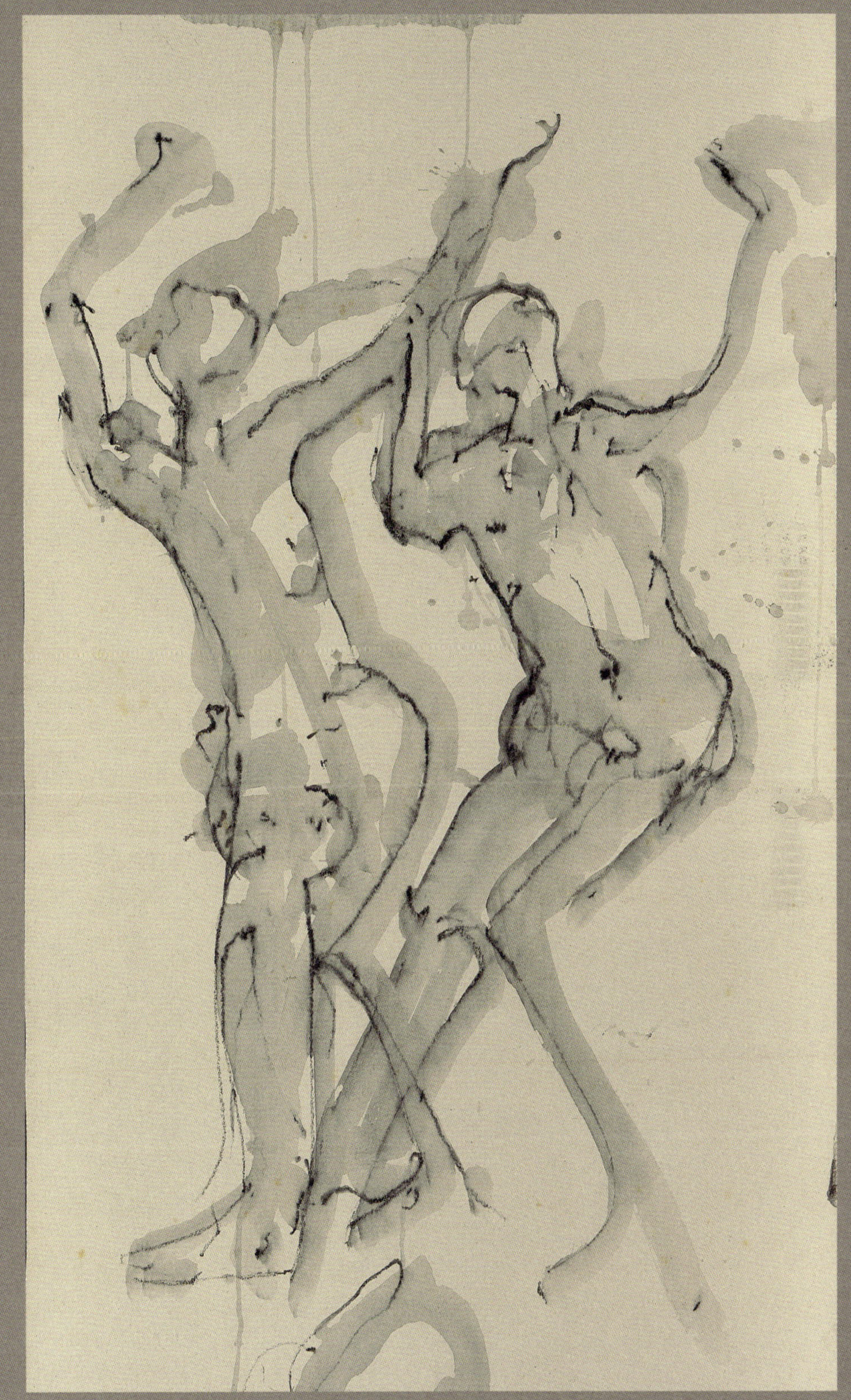

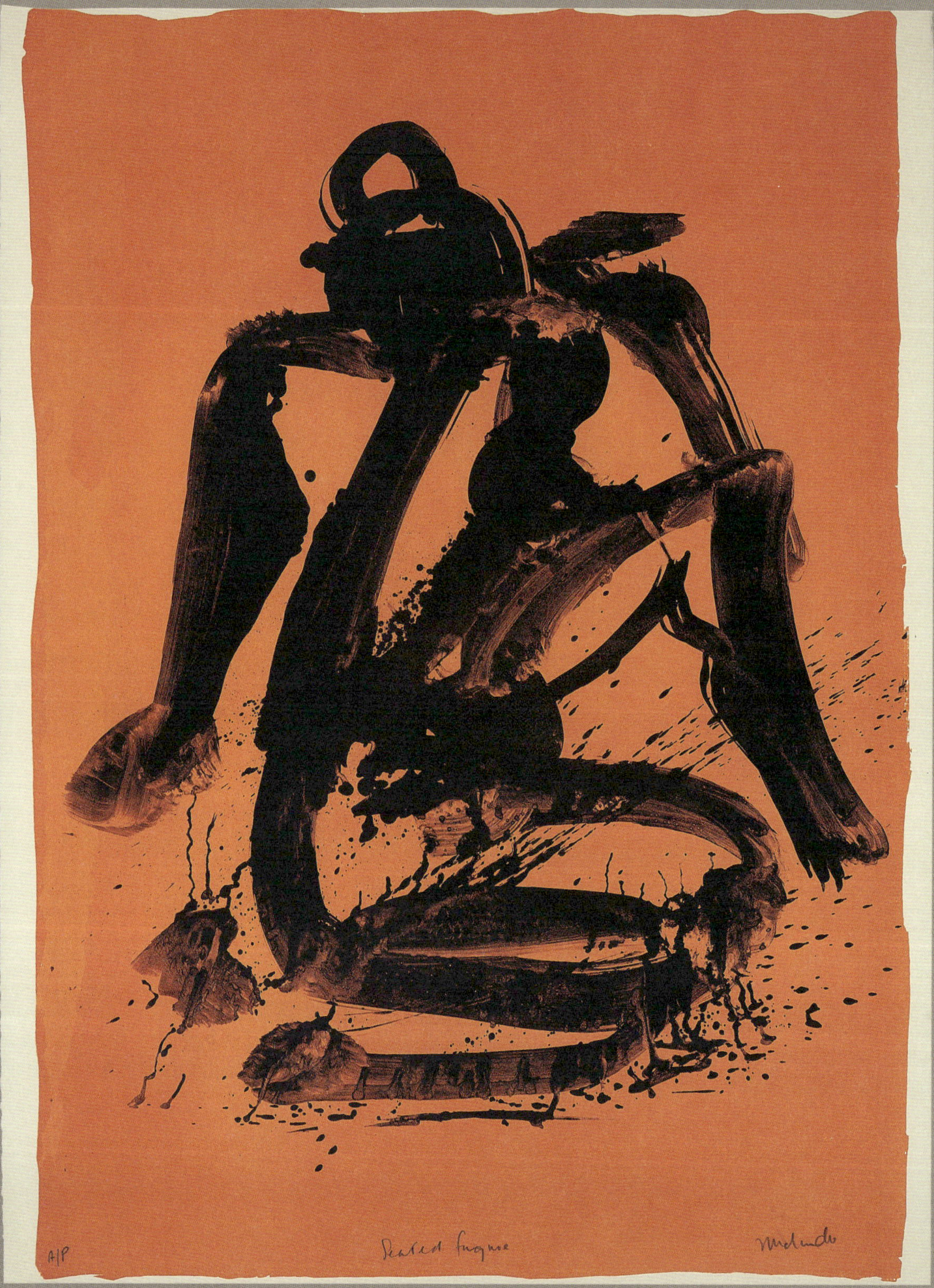

A/P
Seated figure
Melendo

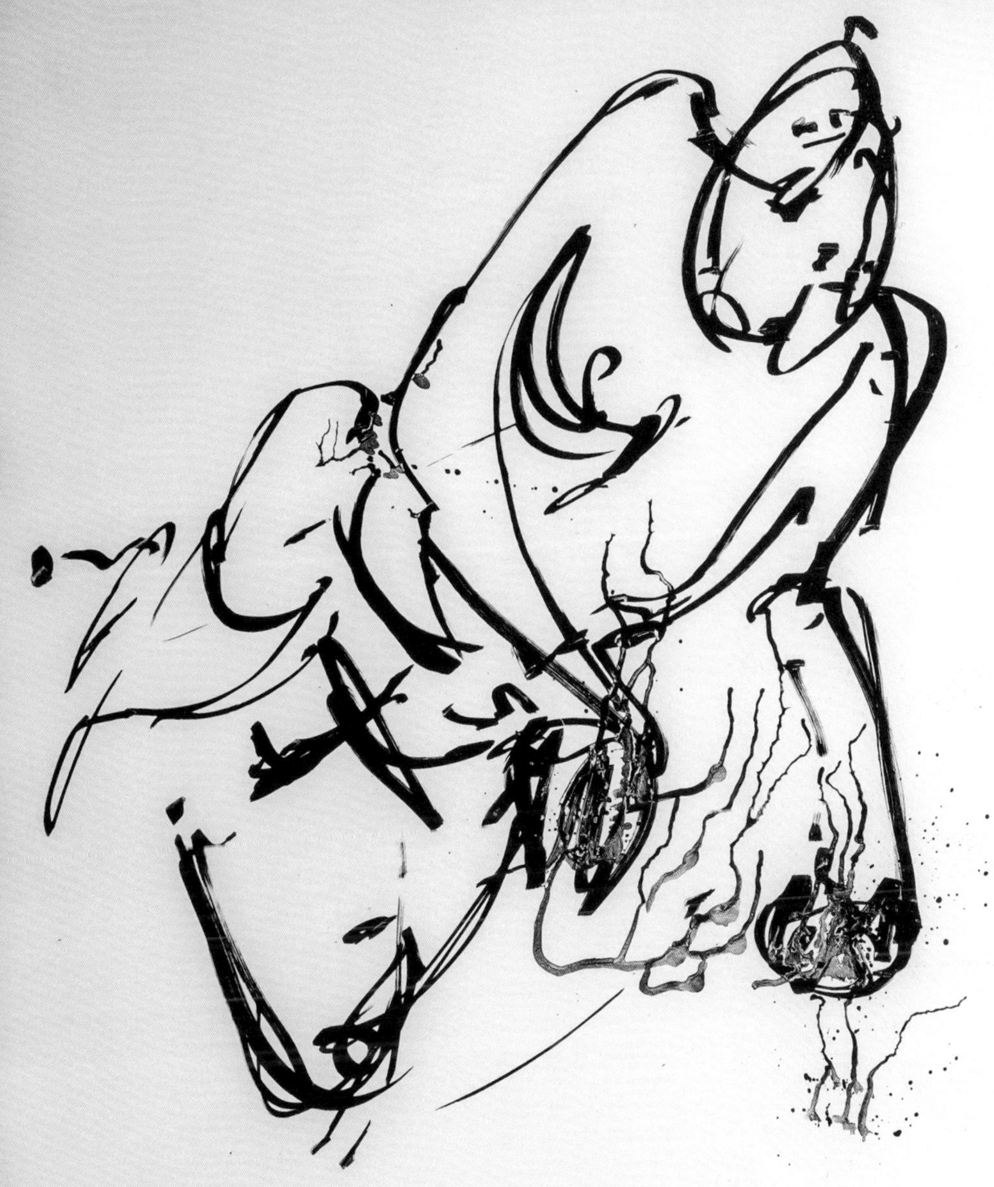

2/4   Seated figure iii   Modudo

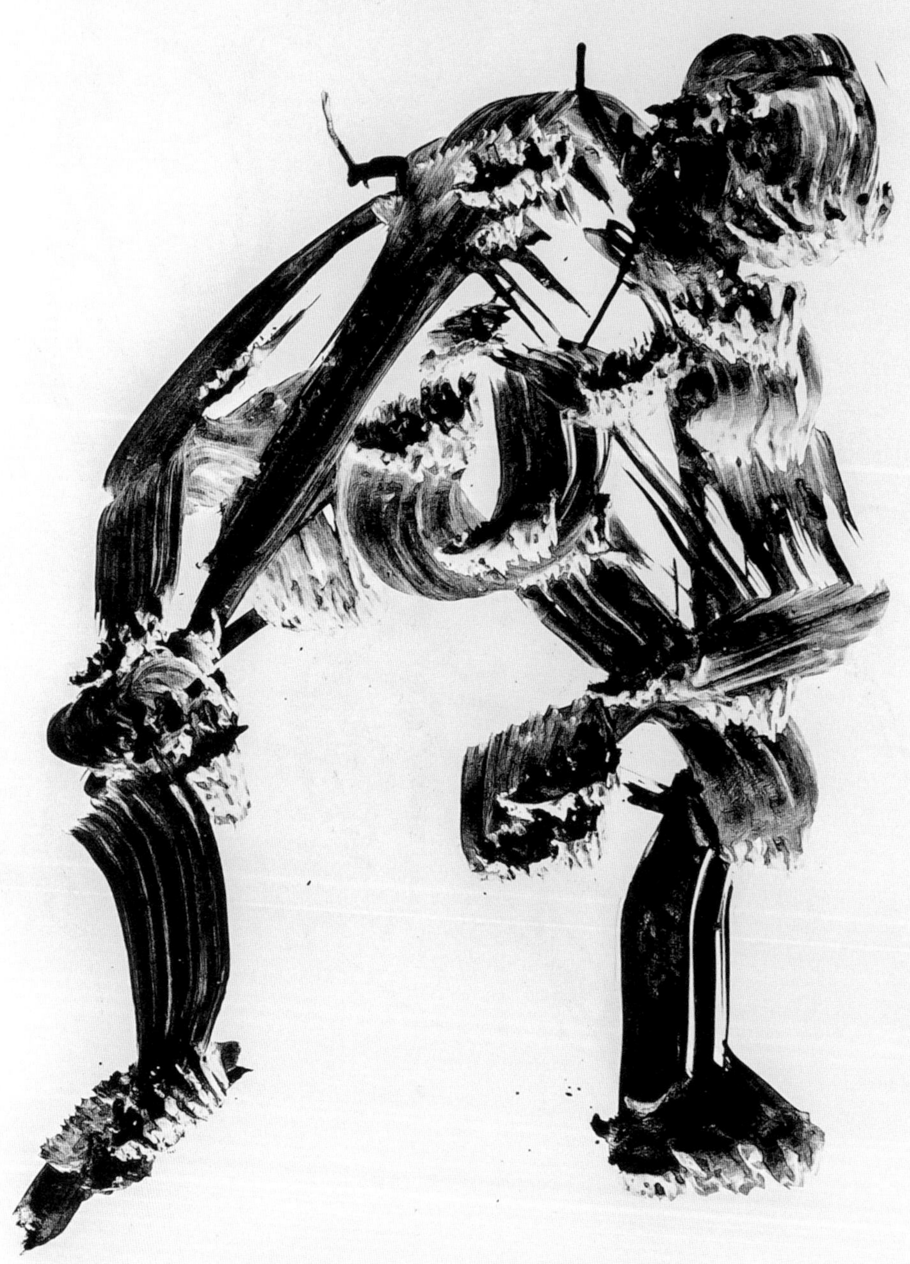

1/2

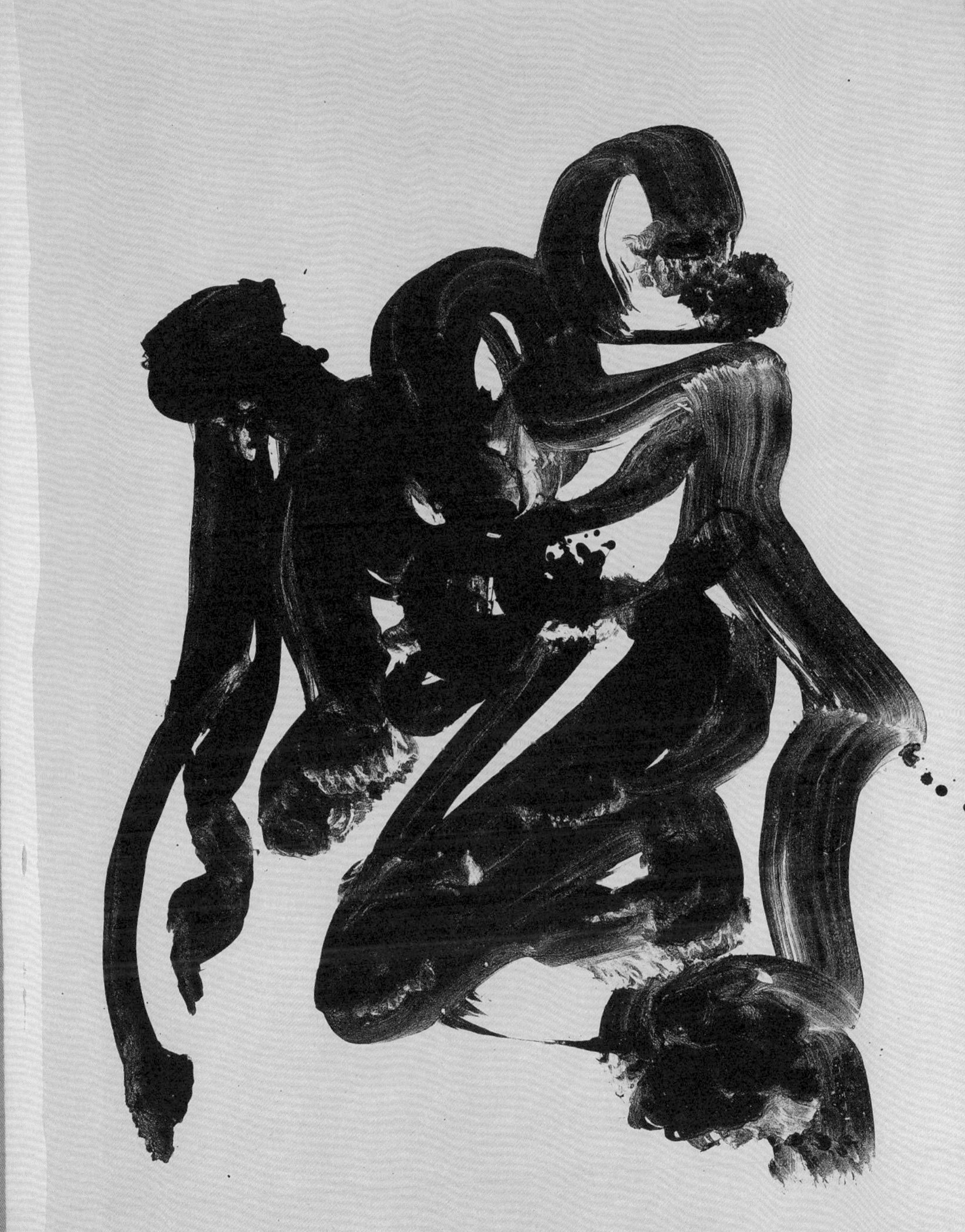

1/2
"Twist"
modundo

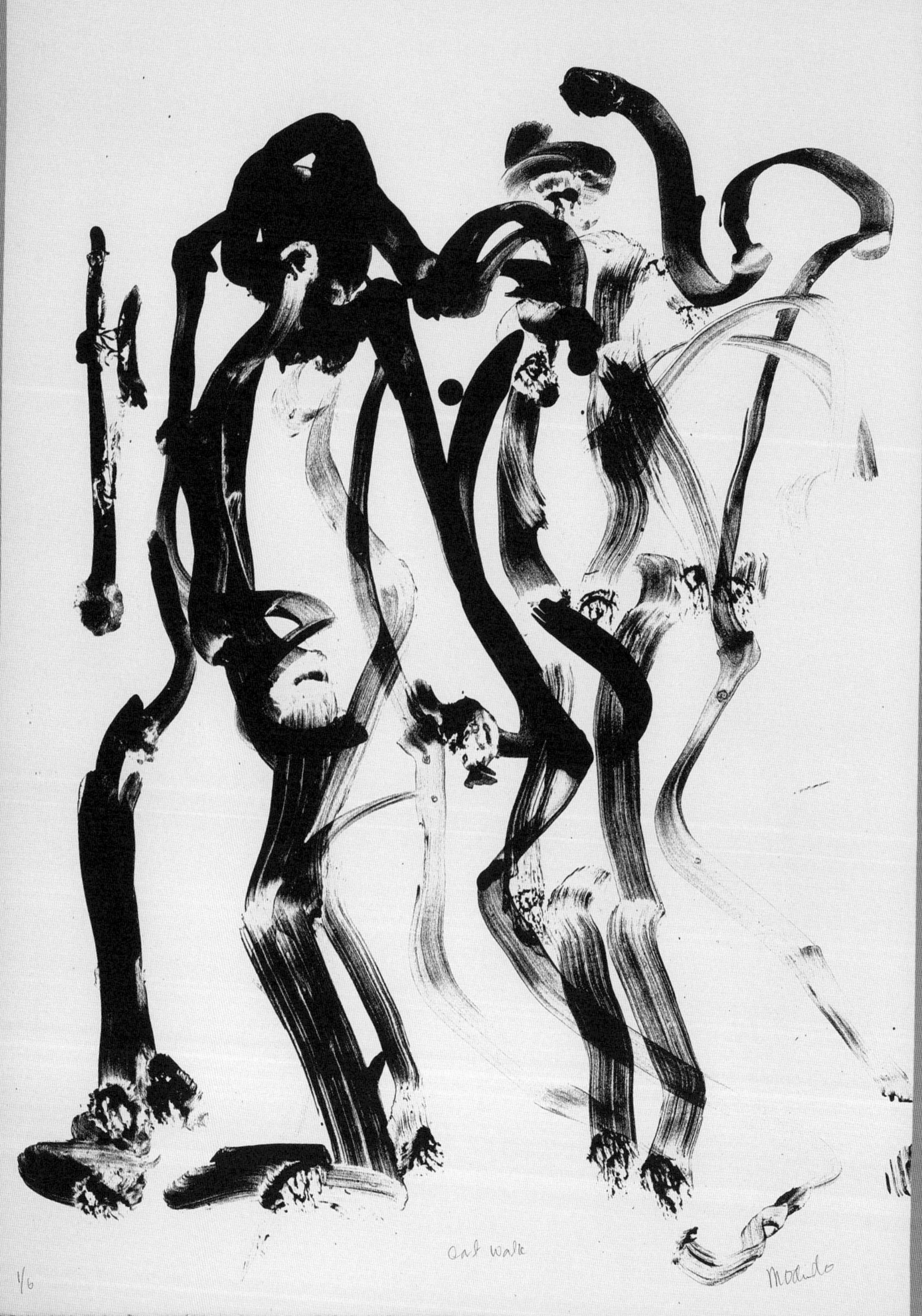

1/6
Oat Walk

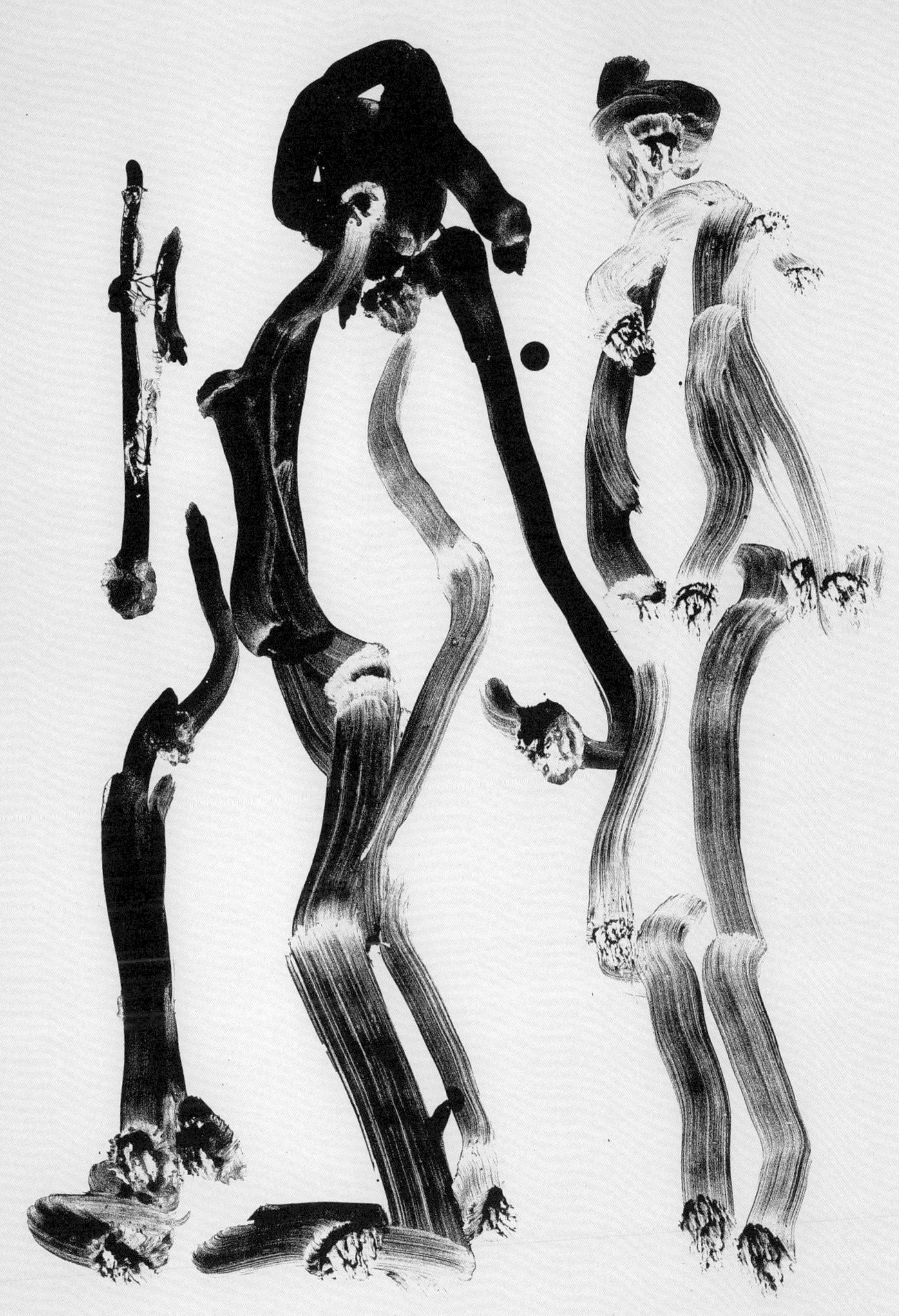

"Cat Walk (1)
½
modudo

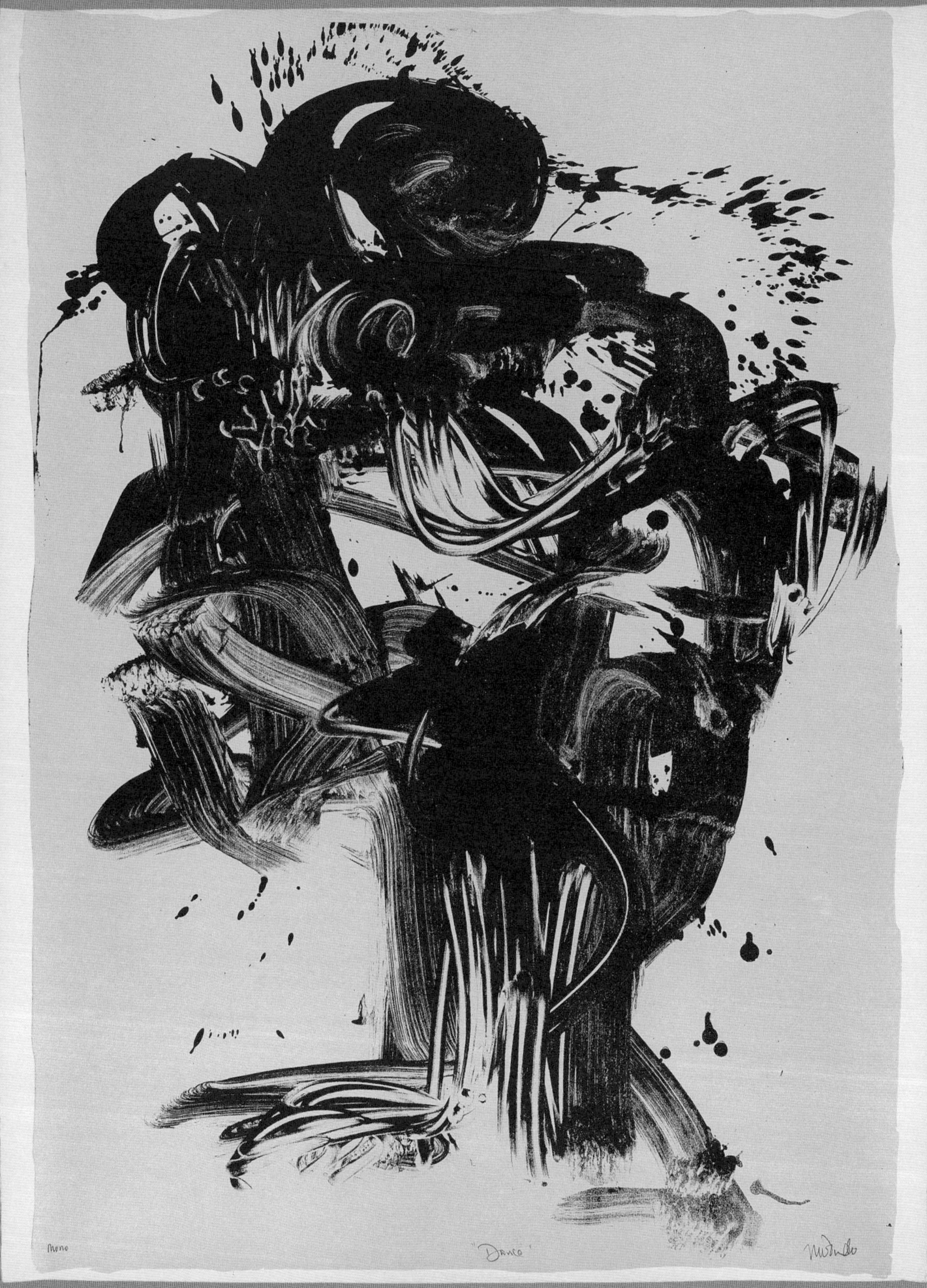

mono
"Dance"

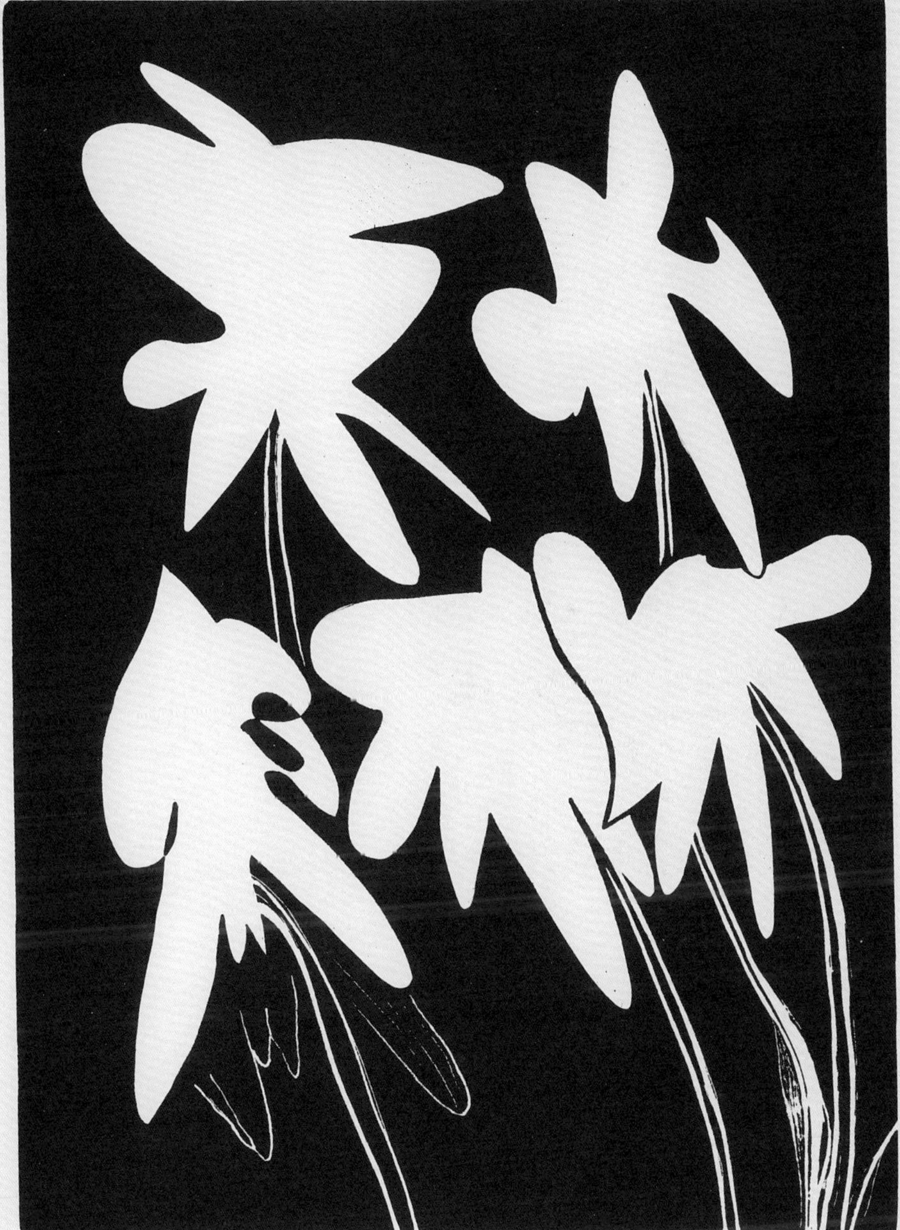

A.P. 1/2
"Spring"
M Odundo
Pilchuck 2011

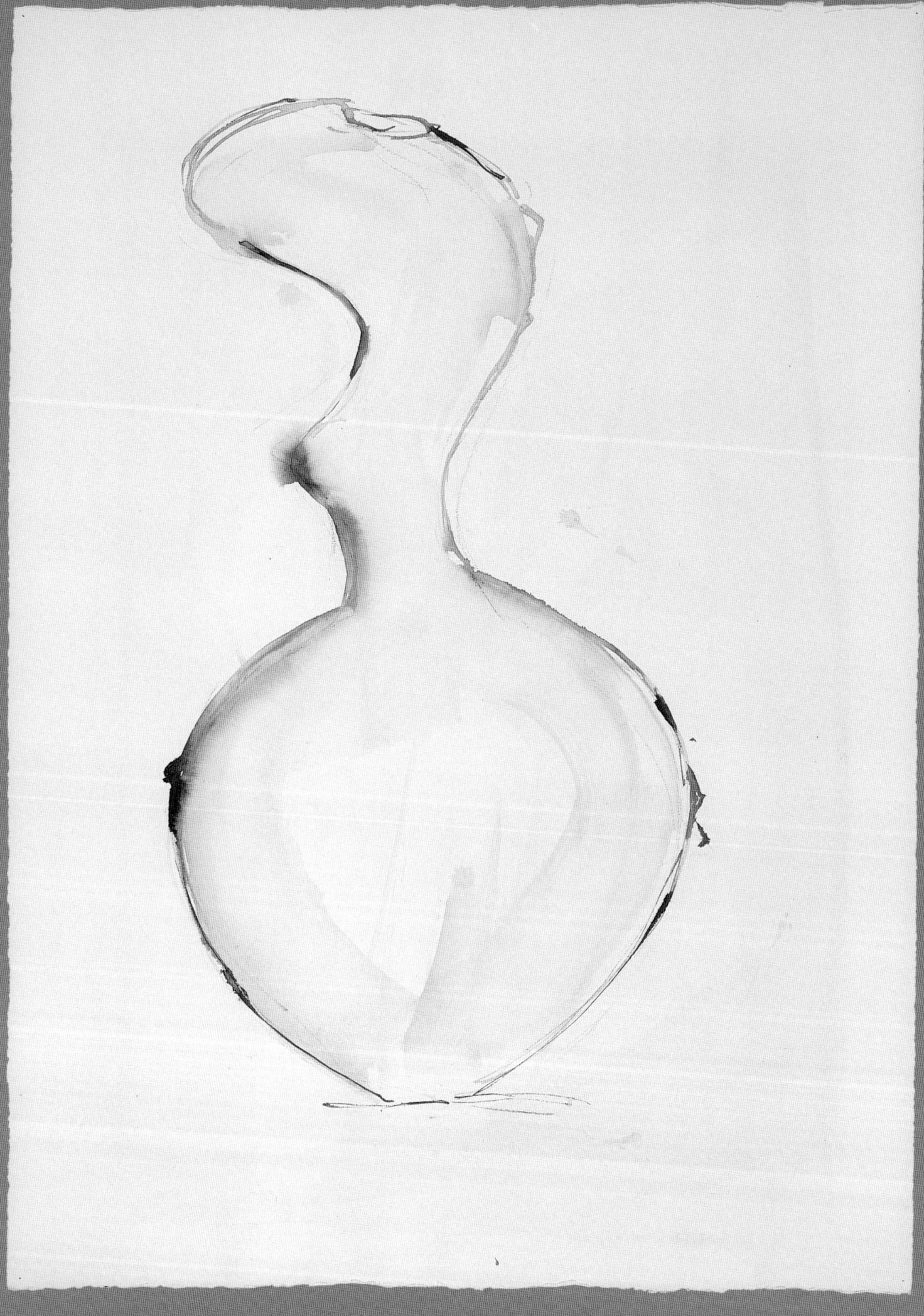

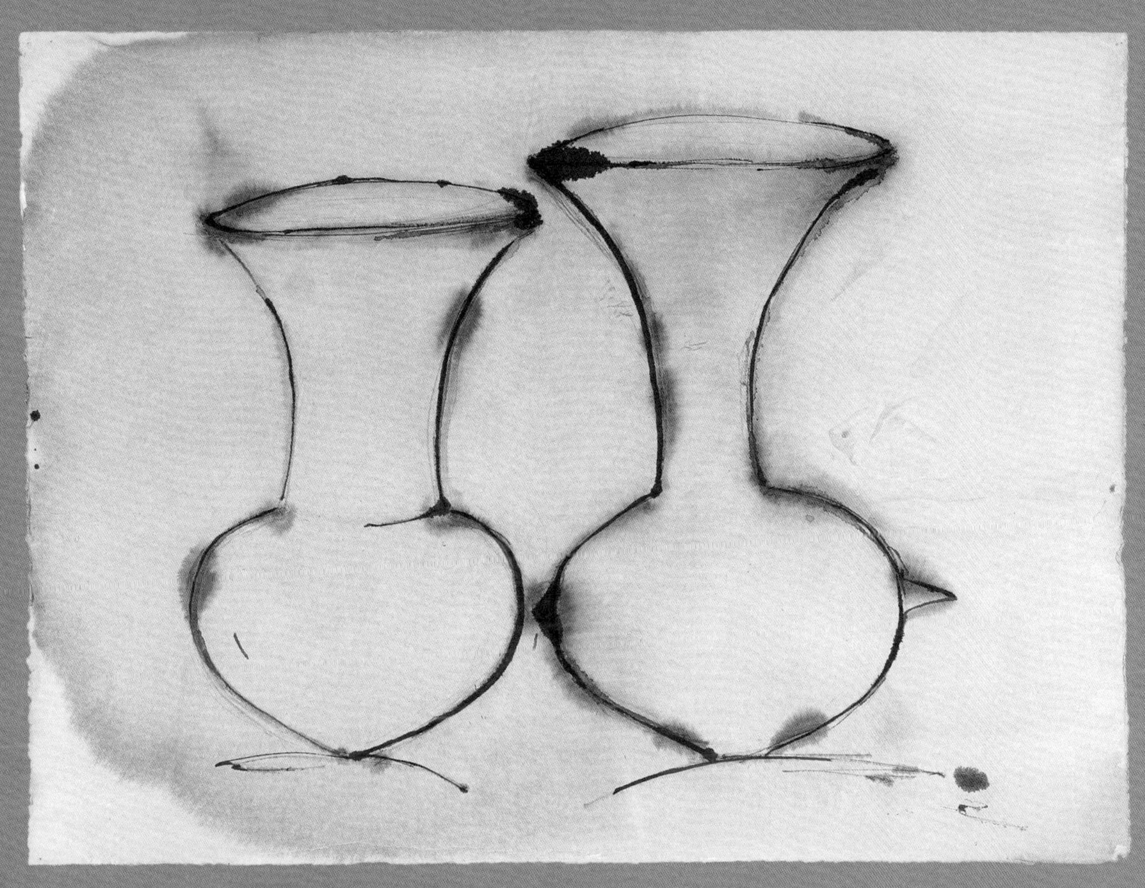

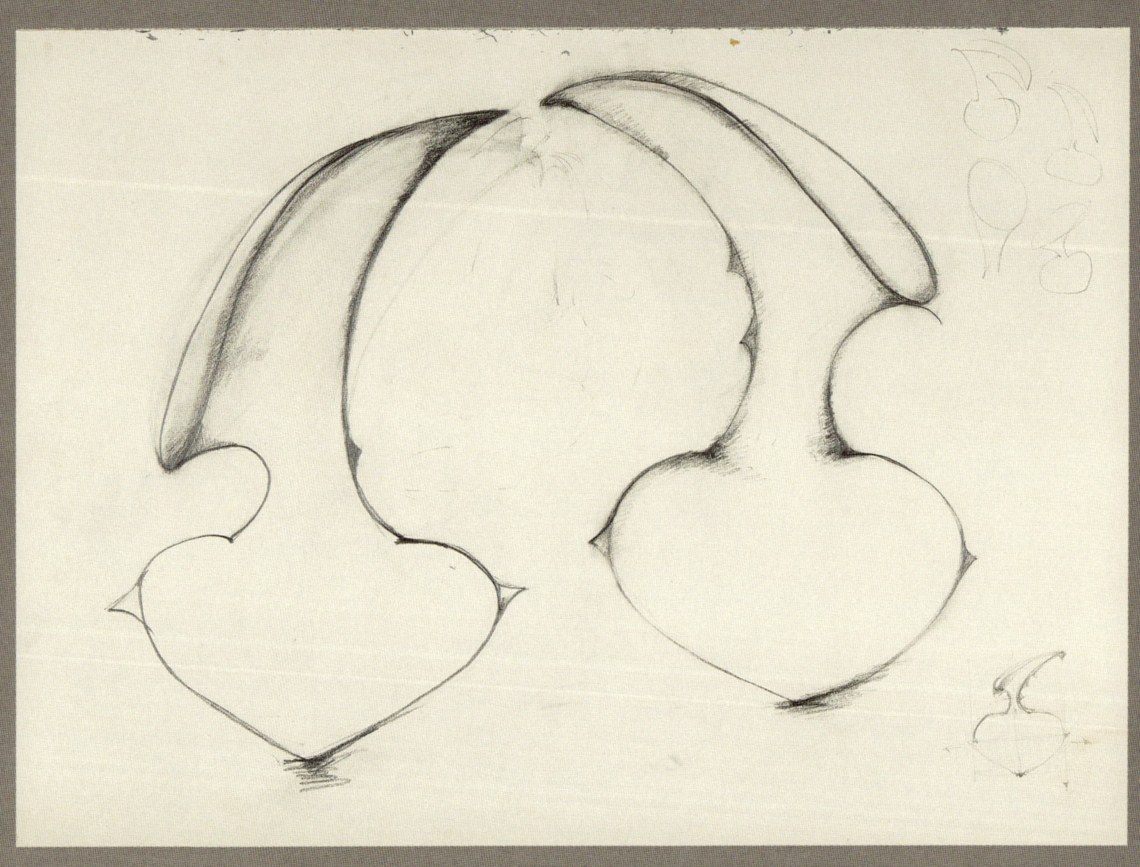

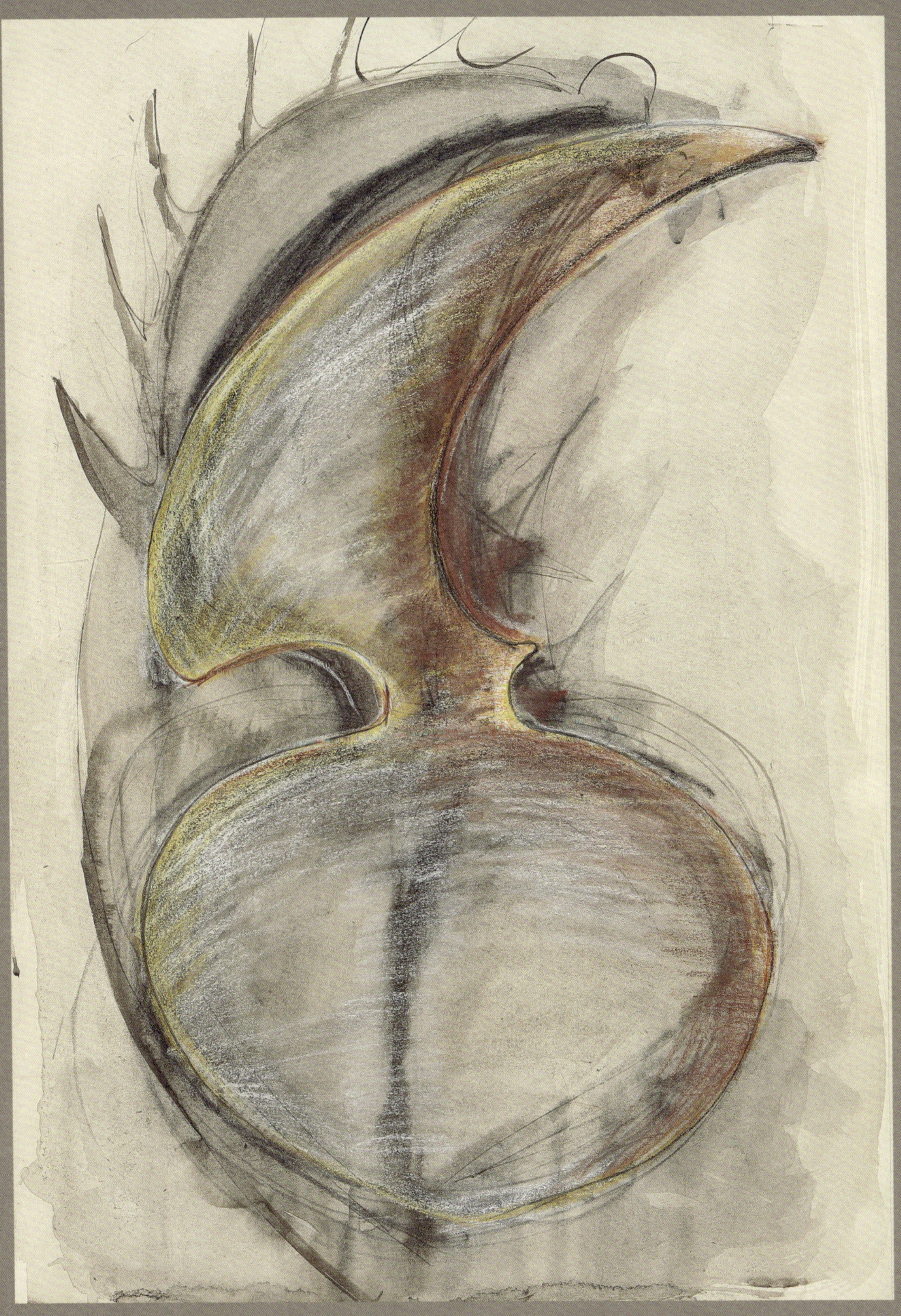

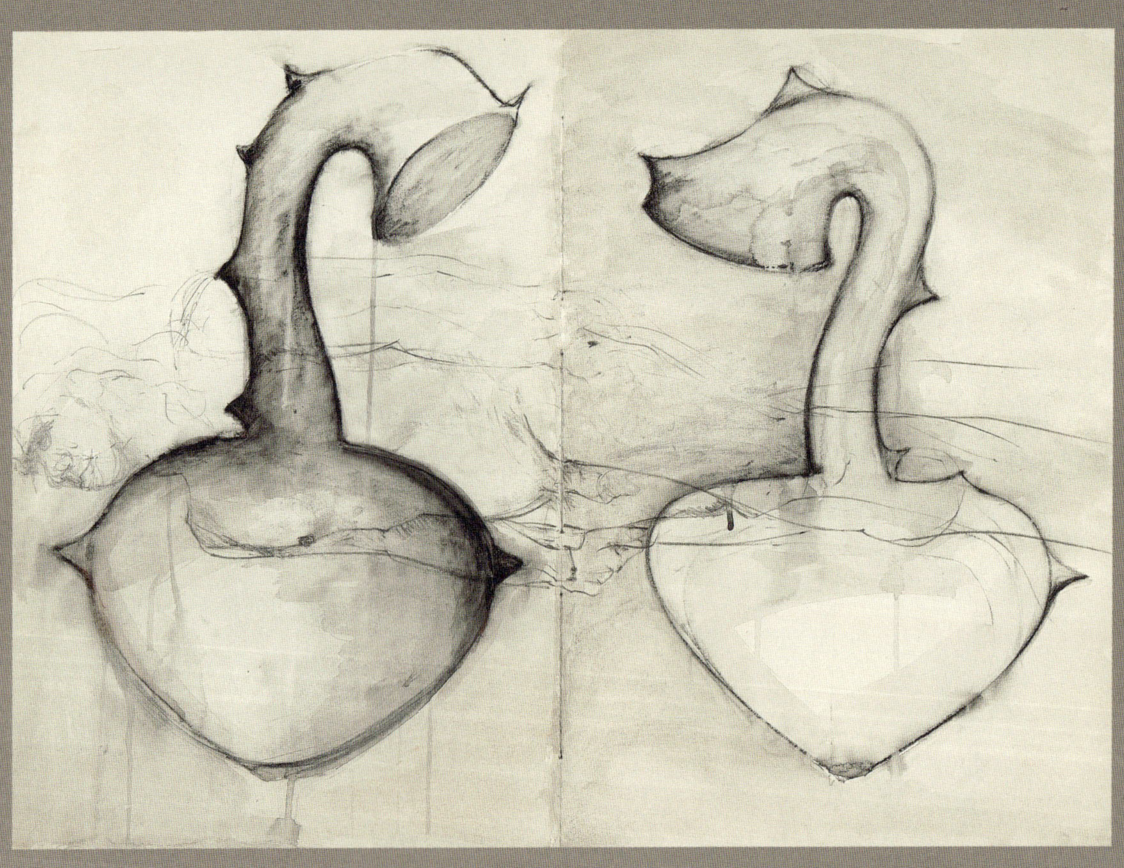

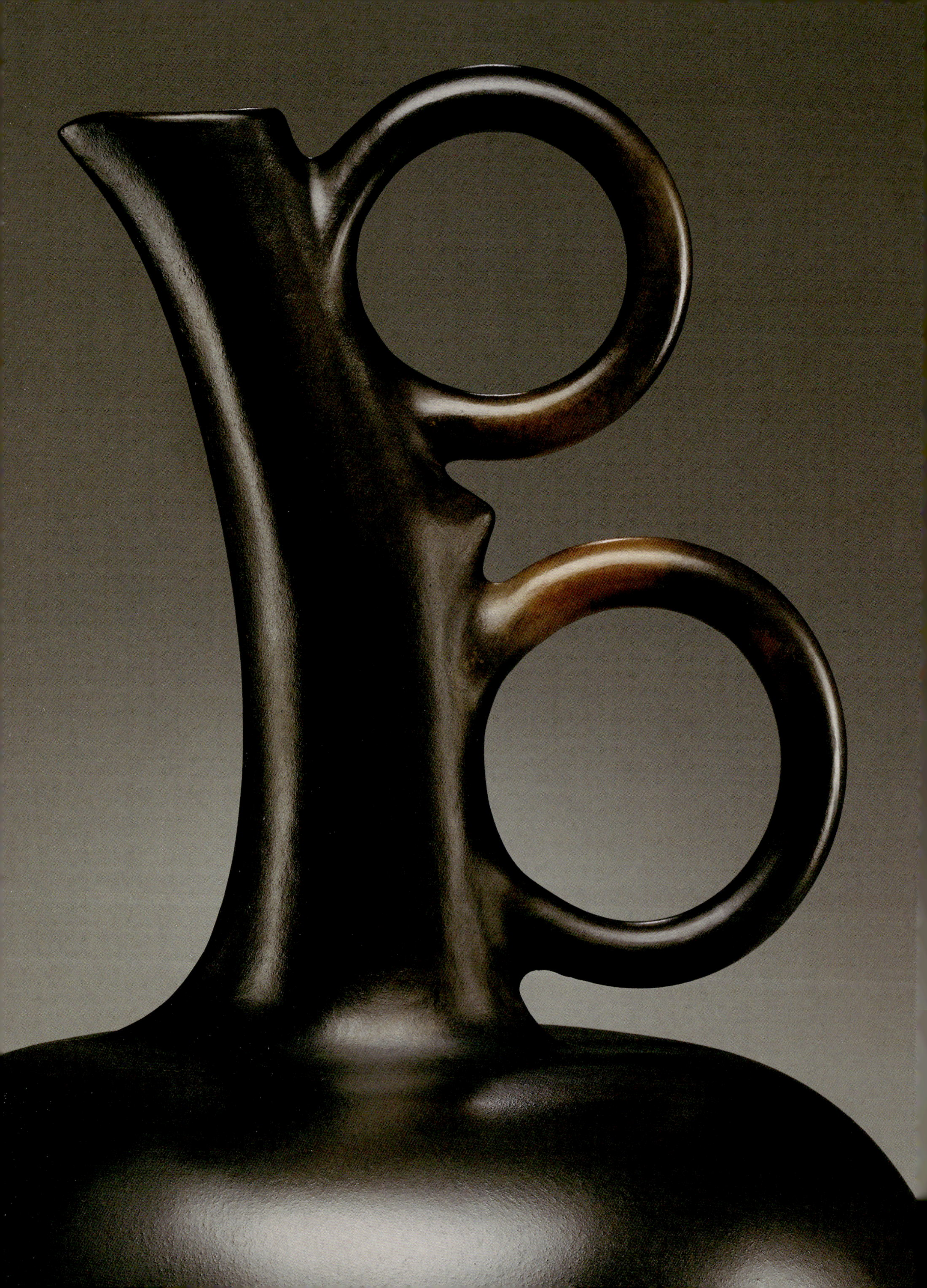

Contributors

Nehal El-Hadi, PhD, is a writer, editor, and researcher. She has a master's degree in environmental studies from York University and a PhD in planning from the University of Toronto. Her research investigates the relationships between people, materials, technologies, and places. El-Hadi lives in Toronto, where she is the editor in chief of *Studio*, a biannual magazine dedicated to contemporary Canadian craft and design.

Elizabeth Harney, PhD, is a curator and researcher in art history and visual culture at the University of Toronto, where she teaches histories of African modernism, anti-colonialism, and postwar visual cultures. Harney was the inaugural curator of modern and contemporary arts at the National Museum of African Art, Smithsonian Institution. Her research focuses on histories of global modernism and contemporary African and diasporic artistic practices.

Educated at the University of California at Berkeley, the University of Vienna, and the University of California at Davis, **Susan Jefferies** established the Gardiner Museum's contemporary ceramics collection and gallery, and was its curator for ten years. As well, she established the Museum's Education and Public Programmes Departments. Noteworthy exhibitions include *Ceramic Modernism: Hans Coper, Lucie Rie and Their Legacy*; *Jean-Pierre Larocque: Clay Sculpture and Drawings*; and *Clay Portraits: Gertraud Möhwald*. She is currently senior advisor to the Mingei Film Archive Project, dedicated to the restoration of films on the history of pottery making.

Sequoia Miller, PhD, is the chief curator and deputy director of the Gardiner Museum of Ceramic Art in Toronto. He holds a PhD in the history of art from Yale University; an MA from the Bard Graduate Center; and a BA from Brandeis University. Recent curatorial projects at the Gardiner include *Shary Boyle: Outside the Palace of Me* (2021) and *Ai Weiwei: Unbroken* (2019). Miller recently co-authored *Ceramic Art* (Princeton University Press, 2023) and was a contributing author to *Simone Leigh* (Institute of Contemporary Art, Boston, 2023). He has taught at the University of Toronto, Rhode Island School of Design, and Yale University. Previously, he was an award-winning ceramist who exhibited and led workshops across the United States.

Barbara Thompson, PhD, is an independent art historian, curator, and art consultant specializing in African art. She served as curator of the Arts of Africa and the Americas at the Cantor Arts Center at Stanford University and as curator of African, Oceanic, and Native American Collections at the Hood Museum, Dartmouth College. She has curated more than forty exhibitions and authored several publications, including *African Ceramics: From the Collection of Franz, Duke of Bavaria* (2019) and *Black Womanhood: Images, Icons, and Ideologies of the African Body* (2006).

List of Figures

Fig. 27 Magdalene Odundo (b. 1950),
Untitled, 1990. Ceramic, 35.2 × 24 ×
24 cm. National Museum of African Art,
Smithsonian Institution, museum
purchase, 91-4-2

Fig. 28a Oluseye (b. 1986), *Ploughing
Liberty #18*, 2021. Found farm tool, hockey
stick, brass dowel, 178 × 23 × 24 cm.
Dr. Kenneth Montague | The Wedge
Collection, Toronto

Fig. 28b Oluseye (b. 1986), *Ploughing
Liberty #16*, 2021. Found farm tool, hockey
stick, brass dowel, 178 × 20 × 20 cm.
Collection of John Donald, Toronto

Fig. 29 Magdalene Odundo (b. 1950),
Untitled, 1997. Ceramic, 36 × 43 × 43 cm.
Maxine and Stuart Frankel Foundation for
Art, Bloomfield Hills, MI

Fig. 30 Magdalene Odundo (b. 1950),
Untitled, 2009. Ceramic, 43 × 36 × 36 cm.
Courtesy of the artist

Fig. 31 (two views) Magdalene Odundo
(b. 1950), *Untitled*, 1987. Ceramic, 37 ×
22 × 22 cm. Maxine and Stuart Frankel
Foundation for Art, Bloomfield Hills, MI

Fig. 32 Unknown artist, *Jebena* (a
traditional Sudanese coffee pot owned by
Nigoumi), undated. Earthenware, 20.3 ×
14 cm. Siddig el Nigoumi's Collection

Fig. 33 Magdalene Odundo (b. 1950),
Untitled, 1995. Ceramic, 51 × 29 × 29 cm.
Maxine and Stuart Frankel Foundation for
Art, Bloomfield Hills, MI

Fig. 34 Zeers ready for sale on display at
market, Omdurman, Sudan, 2010

Fig. 35 Siddig el Nigoumi (1931–1996),
Jebena (Sudanese coffee pot), 1959.
Porcelain stoneware with cane handle,
height 24 cm

Fig. 36 Magdalene Odundo (b. 1950),
Untitled, 2020. Ceramic, 56 × 36 × 33 cm.
Private Collection, New York

Fig. 37 Magdalene Odundo (b. 1950),
Untitled, 1995. Ceramic, 43.2 × 28 ×
28 cm. Yale University Art Gallery. Gift of
Jane and Gerald Katcher, LL.B. 1950

Fig. 38 View of *Magdalene Odundo. A
Dialogue with Objects* exhibition, held at
the Gardiner Museum 2023–2024,
curated by Dr. Sequoia Miller, in
collaboration with Magdalene Odundo.
Exhibition design SOCA Studio; graphic
design Noel Nanton, typotherapy

*Artworks were included in the exhibition
*Magdalene Odundo: A Dialogue with
Objects*, presented by the Gardiner
Museum October 19, 2023–April 21, 2024

Acknowledgements

This publication and the exhibition that occasioned it have depended on the invaluable support and contributions of many people. For their generosity and vision, we thank the Exhibition's Presenting Sponsors: Mary Janigan & Tom Kierans; the Reitberger Family in honour of Renate Reitberger; and Noreen Taylor & David Staines. We also extend our gratitude to the Ontario Cultural Attractions Fund and our Exhibition Supporters: David Binet; the Linda Frum & Howard Sokolowski Charitable Foundation; McCarthy Tetrault; and Power Corporation of Canada.

We thank the institutions who loaned works to the exhibition and the dedicated staff who facilitated that process: Keely Orgeman, Lynne Addison, and Ashley Kane at the Yale University Art Gallery; Yao-Fen You and Antonia Moser at Cooper Hewitt, Smithsonian Design Museum; Dana Moffett and MJ Hagan at the National Museum of African Art, Smithsonian Institution; and Elizabeth St. George, Annissa Malvoisin, and Ernestine White-Mifetu at Brooklyn Museum.

We are extremely grateful to Maxine and Stuart Frankel at the Maxine and Stuart Frankel Foundation for Art for their generosity, and to Benjamin Teague for his work on behalf of the Foundation.

Thank you to Jeanne Greenberg Rohatyn and Andrew Blackley of Salon 94; Emma Da Costa of Thomas Dane Gallery; Greta Bertram of the Craft Study Centre; and Alexandra Burr.

The exhibition included contextual objects, several of which are reproduced here, presented in conversation with the work of Magdalene Odundo. Thank you to the institutional lenders and their dedicated staff who made these dialogues possible: Julie Crooks, Caroline Shields, Alexa Greist, and Donna Austria at the Art Gallery of Ontario; Roxane Shaughnessy and Esther Knegt at the Textile Museum of Canada; and Silvia Forni, Paul Denis, Tracey Forster, Molly Minnick, Melissa Thompson, and Jean Dendy at the Royal Ontario Museum. We are grateful to the private lenders whose works are also reproduced here: Dr. Kenneth Montague of the Wedge Collection; John Donald; and Eleanor Johnson and David Mirvish of the Audrey and David Mirvish Collection.

Thank you to Hugh Freund and Sandra Wijnberg for sponsoring this publication.

At the Gardiner Museum, we are grateful for the support of Executive Director & CEO Gabrielle Peacock, Miranda Disney, Christina MacDonald, Jack McCombe, Karine Tsoumis, Rachel Weiner, and the full Gardiner Team. We owe much of the organization and clarity brought to this project to Ashley Raghubir, Curatorial Research Assistant. We offer endless thanks to Exhibitions Manager, Natalia Goldchteine, whose attention to detail and good humor have been critical.

We are grateful to our external publication partners for their skill and dedication: Michelle Piranio; Ryan Polich, Gina Broze, and Melissa Duffes at Marquand Books; and Michelle Komie, Annie Miller, and Ruthie Rosenstock at Princeton University Press.

Thank you to Elizabeth Harney, Nehal El-Hadi, Sue Jefferies, and Barbara Thompson for their insightful contributions to this book.

Above all, thank you to Dame Magdalene Odundo for her generosity, warm spirit, and wisdom over more than two years of conversations and meetings. It has been an extraordinary gift to work with her.

On a personal note, I thank my friends, family, and the many people who have helped bring me back to good health over the last year, enabling this book to be completed.

Photography and Copyright Credits

All images of artworks by Magdalene Odundo are © Magdalene Odundo. Every effort has been made to contact and credit accurately the sources and copyright holders of the images reproduced in this book. The publisher would be grateful if notified of any errors or omissions to this list that may be amended for future reprints and editions.

Fig. 1, 13, 15, detail of Fig. 15, 29, 31, alternate view of Fig. 31, 33: Photos by PD Rearick

Fig. 2: © Estate of Ladi Kwali, Gardiner Museum, Toronto

Fig. 3, 24: Courtesy of ROM (Royal Ontario Museum), Toronto, Canada. Photo by Gardiner Museum

Fig. 4: Gardiner Museum, Toronto

Fig. 5, alternate view of Fig. 5, 38, cover front, cover back: Gardiner Museum, Toronto. Photo by Jack McCombe

Fig. 6: Courtesy of ROM (Royal Ontario Museum), Toronto, Canada. ©ROM

Fig. 7: Photo © AGO

Fig. 8: © 2023 Helen Frankenthaler Foundation, Inc. / Artists Rights Society (ARS), New York

Fig. 9, detail of Fig. 9: © Cooper Hewitt, Smithsonian Design Museum / Art Resource, New York

Fig. 10: © Estate of Josef Albers / CARCC, Ottawa (YEAR). Photo: AGO

Fig. 11: Photograph by John Martin

Fig. 12: © The Estate of Denyse Thomasos. Gardiner Museum, Toronto. Toni Hafkenscheid Photography

Fig. 14: Brooklyn Museum

Fig. 16, 19, 22, 23, 25, 39, 40, 41, 42, 45, 46, 47, 48, 49, 50, 51, 52, 53, 54, and detail of Fig. 54: David Westwood Photography

Fig. 17: © 1994 Magdalene Anyango N. Odundo, Photograph by Franko Khoury, National Museum of African Art, Smithsonian Institution

Fig. 18, 20, 36: Image courtesy of the artist and Salon 94. Photo by Dan Bradica

Fig. 21: Image courtesy of the artist and Salon 94. Photo by Jon DeCola

Fig. 26: © Eddy Firmin, Gardiner Museum, Toronto

Fig. 27: © 1990 Magdalene Anyango N. Odundo, Photograph by Franko Khoury, National Museum of African Art, Smithsonian Institution

Fig. 28a, 28b: ©Oluseye. Gardiner Museum, Toronto. Toni Hafkenscheid Photography

Fig. 30: Image courtesy of the artist and Salon 94. Photo by Elisabeth Bernstein

Fig. 32, 35: © Stephen Brayne

Fig. 34: Marcin S. Sadurski / Alamy Stock Photo

Fig. 37, detail of Fig. 37: Yale University Art Gallery

Fig. 43, 44: Gardiner Museum, Toronto. Toni Hafkenscheid Photography

Published on the occasion of the exhibition

Magdalene Odundo: A Dialogue with Objects
Gardiner Museum
111 Queen's Park, Toronto, Ontario M5S 2C7
October 19, 2023 – April 21, 2024

Co-curated by Dr. Sequoia Miller, in collaboration with
Magdalene Odundo, RCA DBE
Organized by the Gardiner Museum, Toronto

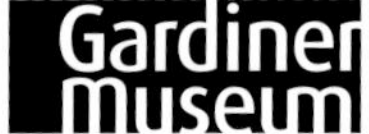 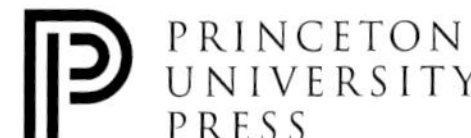

Produced by Marquand Books, Seattle
marquandbooks.com

Edited by Sequoia Miller
Designed by Ryan Polich
Typeset by Tina Henderson, Miko McGinty Inc.
Proofread by Jill Twist
Printed and bound in China by Artron Art Printing

Publication Sponsors
Hugh Freund and Sandra Wijnberg

Published by
Gardiner Museum
111 Queens Park
Toronto, ON
M5S 2C7, Canada
gardinermuseum.on.ca

Published in association with
Princeton University Press
41 William Street
Princeton, New Jersey 08540
99 Banbury Road
Oxford, OX2 6JX, UK
press.princeton.edu

Library of Congress Control Number: 2024932063
ISBN: 978-0-691-26530-8
British Library Cataloging-in-Publication Data is available
10 9 8 7 6 5 4 3 2 1

Library and Archives Canada Cataloguing in Publication

Title: Magdalene Odundo : a dialogue with objects / edited by
  Sequoia Miller.
Other titles: Dialogue with objects
Names: Miller, Sequoia, editor. | Container of (work): Odundo,
  Magdalene. Pottery. Selections. | George R. Gardiner Museum of
  Ceramic Art, publisher, host institution.
Description: Catalogue of an exhibition held at the George R.
  Gardiner Museum of Ceramic Art from October 19, 2023 to
  April 21, 2024.
Identifiers: Canadiana 20240338677 | ISBN 9780691265308
  (hardcover)
Subjects: LCSH: Odundo, Magdalene—Exhibitions. | LCGFT:
  Exhibition catalogs.
Classification: LCC NK4210.O37 A4 2024 | DDC 738.092—dc23

Images
Cover front, cover back: Magdalene Odundo, *Untitled*, 2003.
Ceramic, 47.5 × 25.7 × 26.8 cm. Gardiner Museum. Donated in
loving memory of Susanne Louise Roberts ("Bede"), a fellow
potter, by Camille, Daniel, and Neal Roberts. G06.1.1 ©
Magdalene Odundo
Page 2: Detail of Fig. 15
Page 4: Detail of Fig. 54
Page 8: Detail of Fig. 9
Page 36: Detail of Fig. 18
Page 56: Detail of Fig. 36
Page 70: Detail of Fig. 20
Page 90: Detail of Fig. 37